I'll Meet You At The Lost And Found

A guide to living from the context
of your Inner Self

I'll Meet You At The Lost And Found

A guide to living from the context of your Inner Self

Sam Glory

BOOKS

Winchester, UK
Washington, USA

First published by O-Books, 2019
O-Books is an imprint of John Hunt Publishing Ltd., 3 East St., Alresford,
Hampshire SO24 9EE, UK
office1@jhpbooks.net
www.johnhuntpublishing.com

For distributor details and how to order please visit the 'Ordering' section on our website.

Text copyright: Sam Glory 2018

ISBN: 978 1 78904 030 2
978 1 78904 031 9 (ebook)
Library of Congress Control Number: 2018931102

A CIP catalogue record for this book is available from the British Library.

Design: Stuart Davies

Printed and bound by CPI Group (UK) Ltd, Croydon, CR0 4YY, UK

We operate a distinctive and ethical publishing philosophy in
all areas of our business, from our global network of authors to
production and worldwide distribution.

Contents

Preface: On your horse Spartacus—The Spiritual Warrior

Courage is grace under pressure.
~ E. Hemingway

A new earth in the making

The world is undergoing an all-encompassing transformation that is pushing the individual to shift his focus inward and reclaim the right of innate bliss. On a vibrational level, people are irrevocably starting to understand that contrary to popular belief, happiness is not externally derived, and some friction is bound to be born out of that.

Mainstream news reports notes of chaos and fear with depression as the world's most widespread illness. People are aching more than ever for a fundamental explanation as to who they actually are and what they are meant to be doing within their anthropocentric and ego-ruled societies geared towards violence and self-destruction. But if this general air of malaise could be regarded as the desperate screech of the Inner Self longing to be heard, it would be possible to recognize the strike of the soul as it no longer wishes to live a life out of context. Everything that has been suppressed and denied is gearing up to take center stage, nudging not so subtly to reprogram the entire operating structure as human beings around values that no longer root in the old foundation of fear.

Gaia is undergoing the motions of a new day and luckily for her an increasing amount of people are awakening to discover an essentiality of human development in the conscious relinquishment of the comfort of old paradigms and setting out in an internal search for answers—an act of infinite courage that sees the individual assume a 360° angle of self-responsibility for their life creation. This modern warrior is being recruited to join in the most rebellious act mankind has ever seen: to commit to unconditionally love and respect themselves fully from today on. It will be a silent and internal revolution to break free from the matrix and recognize their true and limitless potential—because only in the absence of unconditional self-love can man be manipulated into creating his prison.

Adamantly armed with an endless thirst for knowledge and unreserved inner strength to carry through the fens of their illusionary self, they are the warriors who won't step down from the evolutionary mountain of self-consciousness. Pushed by an invisible force, they are nudged to look past the illusion of the ego self and reach inwardly for an integrated acquisition of conscious awareness.

This book is for them. To remind them that they are not alone, that they've never been, and that no matter how different or lost they may feel, they are loved—unconditionally so.

Assume the warrior's stance and seek the courage to be aware.

2

Darling, can't you hear me, S.O.S.

All our dreams can come true if we have the courage to pursue them.
~ Walt Disney

Your Inner Self is waiting

Oh, but hello there. How wonderful of you to join me!

Let me put my invisible cigar out and drape my tartan quilt over my legs as you come closer to this astonishing fire I have just lit with the power of imagination. Uh that's nice isn't it? I think I can smell roasted marshmallows and caramelized chestnuts as the snow falls silently on this beautiful winter's evening of your soul. The stars are out and the setting couldn't be more favorable to be with you in this moment of your life and let you know that all of the power, the strength, and all the knowledge that you seek is hidden right inside of your being in this precise moment. That the happiness which you so rightly deserve and seek is never ever in the control of others (this constitutes your family, the politicians, the bus driver or God for that matter), full and absolute control to shape your life can solely stem from within YOU.

The title of this book wants you to remember that. It wants you to know that the part of you that shines, the one that can never truly die, no matter how much you have tried to ignore it or stuff it into the back of your wardrobe, is SOS'ing you right now from some deserted lost and found counter after you involuntarily abandoned it on your voyage—like an old cassette player you no longer needed. After all this time, it's still assured that you will remember it and someday show up and claim it as yours. It's looking at you right now as it's got your attention, slightly smug in its self-confidence that you couldn't get rid of it that easily. So come on then, we need to start working on jolting your memory to where the heck you have left it... the world is a big place you know.

It's time to shut down the ever-imposing noise that surrounds you, the constant distractions that want you to look the opposite way of inwards, the ones that last for a fleeting moment only to leave you with crippling apathy and self-blame. It's time to shift your attention to inside of yourself and pay very close attention, my friend... If you want to see miracles you better roll those sleeves up.

The quieter it is, the more you
can hear within.

3

Baa-baa: The Following Mentality and personal responsibility

We have all a better guide in ourselves, if we would attend to it, than any other person can be.
~ Jane Austen

Going your own way

Let me tell you about Max Hannigan, a dear friend of mine who waited a long time before realizing he had faked most of his happiness around what had been expected by the world instead of walking his own way. He was in his late forties by the time he'd started to sense something was off — working in the typical office environment, married, kids, mortgage, two garages, poodle, you know the crème de la crème with a cherry on top.

He wasn't sad per se, he felt like he had everything, he even believed to like his job — he loved having the money and being revered by his coworkers, his ego adored the attention of a promotion and got frustrated when it didn't get the drip-fed external validation that it needed. He grew on the false sense of security of being settled down and feeling like he fitted in, like he finally had a place in this world, as if he somehow had to *earn* the place! He never realized that just *being* was enough to give him the right to be happy, that it was okay to listen to that side of him that wanted to truly thrive, not just survive. But how could he hear that, after all he had as well as abandoned it to rot in some squalid downtown lost and found corner. The thorny part was his arrogance; his enormous ego had expanded to the size of Greenland and it wanted to hear no bells sounding apparent defeat, even if that actually heralded the acquisition of integrated and unconditional self-love and happiness.

All of his friends pretended to be happy too. They showed up every Sunday for the routine round of golf, proudly boasting about their recent purchases and holidays for everyone to admire. It was this game of *who had more to show compared to others* that had turned them completely deaf to the distant voice of their Inner selves as they continued to give in to their egos. They couldn't find the courage to ask what their hearts truly were yearning for because nobody had told them that it was okay to do so, and the risk of being labeled as different was blood-curdling in the most Scorsese kind of red.

Fitting in is most imperative for those who no longer value their own uniqueness; it hails from the pack animal mentality, right back to cave living. Following the herd has its perks in entry level rationale, or at least it did when we had to wrestle a wilder beast. For one it's safer; flock animals know this, they move following the main authority and do not ask questions as to why they do what they do. They feel the warmth of the bodies around them regardless of whether or not they are heading straight towards a cliff, which brings me to number 2. It's just easier. Following somebody else emancipates the individual from taking any hard-boiled decision. It's the Anti-Ikea mentality for the assembly of life: the pieces here come delivered already made, though the design is often cringe awful and with stains on the seats; any type of following requires less personal responsibility and effort, from following a religion, the world leaders, trends, beliefs. If anything goes wrong (and this is at number 3), the outcome can always be blamed on somebody else because it was never truly your wish or idea in the first place. Playing the game of life as the victim is easy, though the limitations are enormous because the victim never calls the real shots. Once we commit to the courageous act of becoming responsible for our Self, we bring back the power we have bestowed upon our exterior reality by responding to the call of our hearts—and nothing will feel safer than that.

Oh, and what happened to dear old Max, you ask? Well he was eventually struck by a serious case of the soul flu, the one that strikes at midnight and turns you paralyzed from the crown and down. Follow him on his journey as he goes from being the light in the wheelchair to the majestic light of conscious creation.

Tip: Next time you are faced with a choice, ask yourself what your Inner Self really wants, not what everybody else thinks is cool or right for you to do. Your Inner Self always knows best, always has done and always will do. And while you are at it, ask yourself why you would even consider the opinion of others in the first place. Do they define how you feel about yourself?

May your essence burn like
a roaring fire.

4

Being YOU... wait... who? Unconditional self-love

Those who were seen dancing were called insane by those who could not hear the music.
~ Nietzsche

How to integrate unconditional self-love

When we were young we thought the world to be amazing, full of mystery and joyous opportunities. We usually have to get through a lot of our adult lives to half-understand just how right we have been all along, and by then we've already started using Minoxidil for our receding hairlines (or the blue-tinted shampoo for the ladies).

You see, when it comes to self-awareness, often, or should I say always, it's not a case of having to learn new things, but rather unlearn everything we think we know, and remember what was inside us all along, before the mind became corrupted with conditioned and self-limiting thoughts. Before the infamous parasite called fear managed to sneak in and multiply like rabbits in a prairie. It is the chipping away process one must undertake to uncover their true and glorious essence, the masterpiece sculpture waiting to be found underneath all the acquired rubble.

Unfortunately, many people hoard illusions, the false sense of security, the misunderstood notion of being unworthy in the eyes of others if they don't follow what has been laid ahead of them, someone else's expectations, if not their parents' then society's or their culture's. They create a false sense of Self that is rooted in fear and hurt and directly identified with their ego—one where they no longer recognize who they truly are at their core, forever seeking their own inner love and abundance from the mercy of others. Human beings are so desperate to be loved and accepted from the outside which in itself is bordering on farcical given that most people do not know how to love and respect themselves in the first place. Many would go through hell and fire to look for this love externally, several never to return—if only they had known that they didn't have to go anywhere at all.

The slippery aspect is that without unconditional self-love, it isn't possible to achieve personal responsibility. And without personal responsibility, the concept of awareness does not become part of the immediate toolbox, which means that entrusting the power to shape life to the size that best fits the individual is given away to everybody else except to oneself—essentially throwing the right of happiness away for free, just like that, like olive oil down the drain.

People are indoctrinated early on into following restrictive patterns and belief systems and become automatically accustomed to invisible boxes of identity they are certain they need to fit in a society expert in exerting control while imposing limits. You would be a mad man to even question this, after all few people would want to stand alone against the machine.

That's when people start settling for average, more often than not even for mediocre. Because their friend Sally does, their neighbor Dave has done it always, and not to mention their parents who taught them early on that they were loved conditionally, rewarded by their love conditionally, a rule most have carried into their own love relationships as they grew older. Aided by the increasingly fear-based culture, people are taught that a competitive strike is healthy (it could be if self-love was integrated), that it is really still about the crowning of the 'strongest' or the more 'intelligent' or the 'prettiest', although someone, somewhere, has missed introducing the importance of crowning the honor of the most loving. The educational system is often one-dimensional and uniform for all, though everyone is bestowed with individuality and a unique soul expression. Society measures 'intelligence' predominantly by how much information brains are able to hoard, where creative and emotional intelligence is rewarded the least, yet these are the very qualities humanity is yearning for the most.

As soon as self-responsibility becomes an integral part of the individual, it becomes apparent to see that what the world truly needs is more people who can love themselves unconditionally — without this love, life will keep moving out of inner self context and forever be sealed in the grace of something external and unsustainable.

The journey towards the famous unconditional self-love, the one where you don't judge yourself constantly for every thought or action, where you find the will to forgive yourself, where you don't live your life for the acceptance from others because you value and respect yourself first, is the only journey you should consider taking this year. Trust me on that—it will take you to the most exotic and exhilarating places you have ever visited. Remember, who you naturally are is abundant and divine—who you show up as at the party of life is your own image and self-conditioning; when you stop having a problem with who you are, the real you shines through.

Tip: When you have a spare and quiet moment alone, go ahead and hug yourself, as tightly as possible. Hug yourself the way only children do, with your arms close to the neck and face, even if you feel a little silly doing it. Bend your head into your arms and take a real deep breath. Then start this type of dialogue where the inquirer is the three-dimensional you and the responder is your Inner Self. If you feel screwy talking out loud, you can keep the conversation in your mind where you feel absolutely safe. Repeat this Tip every day either in the morning or in the evening for as many days as you can bear it. Let the conversation unfold and progress in the most loving and proactive manner as you learn to be patient and forgiving towards yourself.

> You: Do you love me?
> IS: Yes.
> You: Are you sure?
> IS: Oh, yes, very much so.
> You: But why? I'm so (*enter whatever inadequate feeling you may have about yourself*).
> IS: I love you, unequivocally so. You don't have to be any other way than what you naturally are.

The corner of Max: Max had started to feel an unwonted pull towards his Inner Self, the one he had grown to forget. The first little panic attack struck on that golf course, just as he was about to swing the driver club into the air. Luckily for the fairy of ignorance, however, the whole episode was quickly fixed with a bottle of Coors Light and another strong dosage of self-denial. For now, Max still seemed to be able to keep his act together... for now. After all, his ego was still the master ruler in the Kingdom of those asleep.

You are not here to please others; you are here to be wonderfully you.

5

Mr. Ego, bring me a dream (bung, bung, bung, bung): Observing the ego

The ultimate aim of the ego is not to see something but to be something.
~ Muhammad Iqbal

Taming the ego mind

When the worth of one's being is directly associated with the illusionary perception of identity, it can be very easy for the self-esteem to take a nosedive so deep that a new tenant is forced to move in and restore order. Without further ado, ladies and gentlemen, lords and again ladies, I introduce unto you, the one and only, the Mr. popular right now, Misteeeeeeeer Ego! (Cue the jazz hands and the cymbal sounds.)

Mr. non-integrated Ego is a little magician in the making—all he needs to keep you outside of the light is a curtain, smoke, mirrors and a pretty assistant, which usually come delivered in the form of denial, compensation, fear and distractions—when his hands are moving inside of your mind, don't expect to see a little bunny come tumbling out though, for in his act there is little wonder. He likes to keep you ignorant and a little needy so bringing your awareness into the equation is an essential step in recognizing his shenanigans.

Now, a lot of negativity has been bestowed onto poor Ego. He's not all bad, in fact there is goodness to him if he's to be consciously made your sidekick. With unconditional love, an integrated ego can bring you freedom and even become your right-hand arm to help you shape beautiful things in your life, although all on his own, he cannot, because Mr. Ego is a simple fellow. He does want the same thing as your heart, to be loved, but he is so primitive and a real Neanderthal in emotional intelligence, that he will immediately convince you that brushing all your fears under an invisible carpet of denial is the only solution to keeping strong and successful (ergo to be loved, because you, dear one, didn't keep this end of the deal). Of course, what your ego (and thus your mind) wants is far from what your heart is whispering, so when you pursue and don't achieve all the things in life that your ego wants you to go for, you feel hurt.

Many people live by the belief that their hearts must be tamed because they will lead them astray, or even worse, will get them judged by others, which for their egos is a fate worse than death itself. It's a tricky scenario because once the wings of the Inner Self have been severed, the failsafe parachute (the ego) becomes deployed, and unfortunately without awareness, this uncoordinated fall through life isn't very easy to spot.

Only when we are able to watch our ego from a spectator's standpoint, rather than from a participant's, can we begin to listen more discerningly to the deaf notes in between, the ones that want us to really thrive in our lives, not to just get by — by consciously looking at our ego for the child that it is, we can learn to feel compassion for it and understand why it has fought for our cause so much, and begin a dialogue. You will start to appreciate that all your Inner Self beholds is beautiful and perfect on its own already, without the need for external validation. When you are able to express yourself not for what is tactically advantageous in order to gain something from the outside (ultimately this will always be love), not to set yourself aside for better manipulation of others (again, to feel and receive love), not in fear of what the reaction might be (because all you want is love, love, love), then can you truly speak with genuineness and express the real uncompromised you. If only we had loved ourselves in the first place, the little voice inside us is whispering, life would be so much easier. Time has definitely come for the ego to listen to Dave Brubeck and take 5 while you dive deep.

Tip: Place your hand onto your heart, as if you were holding it. Close your eyes and envision a white string going from your hand and into your heart, connecting the two. Focus on your breathing by inhaling through your nose and exhaling with your mouth. Repeat this three times. Sit in this moment for a few minutes as your mind becomes still. Feel the palm of your hand become warm, the light of your heart pouring into your arm, your body and your mind. You are formally meeting with your heart for the first time. That's cause alone for some bubbly.

The corner of Max: Max was used to feeling like the King of the Castle in his work environment. The ladies turned to jelly at the sight of his biceps and the men looked up to him for being the number one salesman of the decade. When he walked into the office, people would greet him with enthusiasm and excitement; his boss often patted his shoulder for a job well done for everyone to admire. Then one day his boss decided to retire and, unfortunately for Max, the new younger boss did not quite share the same reverence towards him; after all, Max was a bit galling in the personality department (let's just say that kindness was not his middle name). So when his popularity slowly descended from rooftop terrace to lobby level, Max started to feel pain. He couldn't quite explain why he cared so much about the opinions of others, but unbeknownst to him, his ego needed to be validated at all times in order to keep up his charade. Needless to say, a seemingly bleak period lay in the horizon for dear Max.

The bigger your identification with your ego is, the smaller will your awareness of your Inner Self be.

6

Jump, monkey, jump: The Illusory mind

Man is the only creature that refuses to be what he is.
~ Albert Camus

How to still your mind

A lot of the human thought-process is a direct manifestation of the ego mind (thoughts that are grounded in desire and personal needs), so it isn't a surprise that the issues which you see in the world today, be it personal, social or global, have their roots one way or another in this ego thinking.

On average, the human's mind has approximately fifty thousand individual thoughts a day, with many surrounding the same subjects ad nauseam. If you envision these thoughts as a myriad of connecting branches in the jungle of the mind, Buddha's monkey analogy (kapicitta) for the attention of the conscious mind is a very befitting one. Swerving from left to right, right to left over and over again, the untamed little monkey is master at becoming very excitable at external stimuli and giving you little more than a headache and a running commentary of what you already know.

On a practical level, the mind is what sets man aside from his fellow primates in intellectual intelligence—it got him the wheel, electricity, the fitness tracker he got for Christmas and wore twice, and the espresso coffee machines that Clooney likes. Ironically, however, it is also what makes man unique in creating nonexistent problems throughout his day. The human being, unlike any other creature, is able to live with a distorted and often false sense of self that catapults him effortlessly into a state of unhappiness and separation from his inner light—this happens when the mind takes over the duties of the master and forgets his position of the dutiful servant.

The rest of the animal kingdom is an excellent representation of the natural state of being without the ego distraction. When Joe the dog walks down the street on his way to Miss Shih Tzu, he isn't inclined to suddenly stop and think: Wait... what if she isn't going to like my scent? Is she gonna dig or not?? No thought, no problem. Dog simply *is* and he isn't apologetic about it.

The mind loves to create issues, to analyze, to make things harder than they are, as it has nothing else better to do when undisciplined. When the mind is given the sole control of your vessel, you can rest assured that not only will you revel in infinite mind diarrhea, but you will attract unnecessary obstacles on your path that weren't even there in the first place. That's called (in strictly academic terms) a f*cking waste of time.

In today's busy societies, there is no time for much, and certainly none for just *being*. When we arrive home after a really long day of stressful meetings, straining debates, physical exhaustion... you name it, what are we usually inclined to do? We need to switch off sort of speak; we need to think about something else, get distracted, because our thoughts are often driving us crazy. So because we habitually never got into the practice of having full control of our minds, we may turn on our television (or our tablet, laptop, phablet etc). We let the bright and vibrant colors of our LCD screen temporarily hypnotize us into watching somebody else make a fool of themselves, as focusing on the idiocy of others in a reality show will mitigate the perception of our own life and distract us from what our Inner Self is trying to show us. We'll perhaps pour ourselves a glass of wine or open a can of beer so we can properly relax, to get the edge off. And it works maybe, temporarily that is. But the mind is impatient; it's only a toddler stomping in the corners to get our attention as soon as the adverts come back on.

Nighttime descends, and as we prepare to wind down and go to sleep, the untamed thought-process reappears like a majestic racing horse on steroids, examining the next issue at hand while we lay awake at 1AM worried by what it is telling us. Morning time arrives all too soon and then Bang! Hello you, I hope you had a nice night's rest. Now… where were we with all the stuff we need to reanalyze one more time, hey?! And did you think about all of the things that you have on today? What about tonight? What about your meeting tomorrow? And what about the weekend?? Did you think about that???!

The alternative you ask?

Well I'm glad you did. One word: meditation. If you listen very carefully, you can probably hear your brain scream with appalling aversion (after all it knows it means hot water for it). Clever little brain, it got that right. The good news is that you don't have to sit in the lotus position and listen to dolphin sounds, you can meditate anywhere and anyhow it best fits you. Meditation is the quintessential state of being, to be present, but not present with your mind, rather with the absence of it. It allows you to reattain control of who you think you are and add some order to the incessant noise that your mind insists in creating for every second of your existence. You are effectively teaching your mind to be active and present, but on your terms, because a disobedient thought-process will do you no good except burning you out faster than a Roman candle. Eventually it will win, I guarantee you, the mind is very, very strong (just think of how many years of training it has had). That is unless you decide to do something about it and put it in its place right now. Then maybe you will be able to forge a nice relationship and start working in symbiotic partnership. Like on a radio, you will turn down the insanely loud mental noise and instead tune more into the frequency of your soul… they really play beautiful music on that station.

Tip: Close your eyes, and breathe deeply in through your nose counting to 4 and exhale slowly through your mouth counting to 5. Repeat this three times. Feel your body relax from your feet, your calves, your legs, your abdomen, loosen your shoulders and feel the weight on them disappear, just like that. Then relax your eyelids, the muscles in your face, around your lips. Take another real deep breath and focus on this out-of-focus black dot on this huge white canvas. It's tiny, it's really just a small black flicker getting slightly bigger and a little crispier for every second. Just sit there and look at the dot for as long as you can, just that and nothing else. Look at how that dot changes color from black to grey, and back to black again. There are no thoughts associated with that. Nothing but the moment.

The corner of Max: A few months had passed since Max's first panic attack on that beautiful Sunday afternoon. Five others had promptly ensued, usually hitting him at night, drenching him with sweat and desolation as he lay awake staring at the ceiling and feeling more lost than ever. It was on those nights where his restless mind played a rather unfair game of cat and mouse, eagerly challenging him to hide in the corners of his self before his mind caught up. His mind was intrigued, exhilarated even to be able to prove his strength in such a victorious manner; he was the real numero uno, or so he thought. Then Max decided to purchase a mindfulness booklet and it all started to go a little downhill for his monkey from there. Yay!

Your every thought affects your physical reality—create them with love.

7

Where did I leave my keys... and my happiness? Integral contentment

Don't let the behavior of others destroy your inner peace.
~ The Dalai Lama

Happiness is only found within

Ah happiness—the holy grail of humanity. Sought by man since the beginning of dawn, it has been the guiding force to every action and every thought ever made. It has been the carrot to every donkey ride, every feat or accomplishment, and every step ever taken.

The great paradox of this pursuit is that as long as fundamental happiness is searched for on the outside, it will be guaranteed not to be found—it will be the necessity scavenged for on the wrong territory while being ever-present on the *inside*, and in plentiful amounts. The entire practice needs to have its focus internalized and realized as a state of *being* as opposed to *doing*, free from any dependable component. Elemental happiness of the Self is not assailable from your external reality, it just *is*. That's the beauty of our infinite and radiant consciousness.

Though, in today's society, the search for happiness is mostly geared towards hedonistic channels, through desire, pleasure and reward. It's the sugar rush equivalent to a fleeting moment of patchy happiness, the stopgap we're turning into when we believe our stash to be empty. You're feeling sad? Watch the little hand reach straight for the credit card. Feel uneasy? Off you go to the gym and concentrate on your squats instead of asking those questions. Restless or bored? Well social media here we come. Easy peasy. Though they all last for as long as a lousy carousel's ride and will leave you reeling for just a little more. It's a feeding mechanism that isn't very sustainable as it is forever dependable on something external from your Self, a mere reaction to an action, another form of compensation while ignoring your inner Self.

When happiness is searched for, limited beliefs also gallantly swoop in to try and impede you from realizing that your happiness is being purposefully hidden from sight by telling you that to be happy you must work hard, that you should be worthy in the eyes of others or that happiness itself is something which you must have earned in order for you to be guilt-free. You may join the charismatic sales guy who promises you happiness in 10 steps which he has eloquently sold to you so you can finally be in control and take action, though even he is overlooking the limits of the mind in providing you with your inherent bliss. So you roll up your sleeves and construct your vision/goal/dream board (which is really just desire) and set yourself off in the great search. While you walk on this treacherous path, you are met with rain, bitter gale-force winds and you may even get to breaking point because you are not happy on this path; and as you know, if you are not happy on the journey, there is a good question waiting to be asked. When you recognize that nothing in the identification of your ego Self can ever provide you with your elemental energy of happiness, you become free. As always, all you really needed was inside.

Tip: While meditating, try and ask your heart what happens when you take away your labels such as your name, your nationality, your beliefs and all that make up the identification of your persona. You may at first feel as if you are losing your identity, but quite the opposite is actually true as your essence will finally have the space to make itself heard. And that's where the *well of all that is*, is found.

The corner of Max: Max had started to meditate once in a while,

when it all got a little too much at work, or when his wife nagged at him, or his kids demanded too much. He began to sense the benefits of reevaluating the way he was thinking about his life, but he was yet to make that fundamental connection with his Inner Self. His worth was still directly connected with his identity, from how much money he made, how he looked, to where he shopped. Happiness was something he went out in the world to get, not something that already came built-in when he was born. Now the nights didn't seem as bad as the mornings, that moment before he fully awoke to get up and redo the daily parade all over again. He started to feel empty inside, apathetic even; his legs fell heavy against the pavement as he dragged his sorry butt to the coffee shop once more.

Happiness is the platform from where we should do and create, not do or create in order to be happy.

8

Unexpected Item in bagging area, remove this item before continuing: Diseases

All that we see or seem Is but a dream within a dream.
~ Edgar Allan Poe

What does it mean to be ill?

The connection between our physical bodies and our inner selves is one that has puzzled scientists from the beginning of dawn. The first affects the other and vice versa, the question is to what extent? We may blame a virus on our poorly-functioning defense system, which is partly accurate, but deep down we know that our defense system is fueled by how we *feel*. When we don't take care of our Inner Self, diseases swoop in as unwanted guests, and unfortunately once they are in, they are difficult to get rid of (a little like my auntie Shirley).

When we oversee our personal and spiritual growth and desire to truly shine and do what our Inner Self wants us to do, the body protests. It starts out with a cold, it augments that with a nice little bronchitis here and there, and evolves that into a rare case of pneumonia, all just to attract your attention to the fact that you haven't really been truly happy being the assistant manager at *Hamburgers-are-us* for the past thirteen years, and that it is time to give that sculpting class a chance. Negating your heart's voice will only make it louder and louder until it is finally heard, meaning that the next tonsillitis visit is hardly a surprise. All scenarios are of course individual. It is entirely up to the individual to identify the mechanics behind any illness and pain; something that can only be done once a link between mind and heart has been established.

Some people's egos (who will most surely negate this until

the end of their days if confronted) have found a pretty cozy spot in the whole self-pity syndrome and actually revel in the notion of being poorly in an attempt to be loved and taken care of by the people around them. Without an illness, their ego identification would not be able to exist, a cure would take away who they think they are, their actual calling card to be able to have a place in this world. Playing the victim is a great role because it absolves you of responsibility for your life, but it's also a lousy one because it means you can't change anything about it and will forever be locked into the mercy of others. As soon as self-responsibility becomes a habit, illnesses and diseases can be regarded as the messengers that they are. The good news is that once light has been shined upon them, they usually get the memo and go back from whence they came.

The key question is not how to best treat an illness, or even how to prevent it because more often than not we are asking the wrong entity. By directing our conscious awareness towards our inner selves, we discover our ability to understand why we have manifested any illness into our lives in the first place. What is it trying to make us aware of? Sometimes it can be present to motivate, inspire or even tutor us and those around us in ways no other teacher could ever have done. When we realize that everything going on in our existence has been attracted by ourselves, we begin to understand the immense power that we hold. Scary? Sure, it can be at first. Empowering at the same time? I truly hope so.

Tip: Positive thinking is effective, but don't ignore your inner voice. If you are feeling hurt or dissatisfaction, don't automatically dismiss it with ephemeral rainbows. Go deeper, wear your investigative beret and find out what wants to come out. Plastering a fake smile will only subdue the ache for a while. Be that warrior and endeavor to look pain in the eye; you have come this far.

The corner of Max: Growing up, there was nothing Max had wanted more than becoming a veterinary. Limited beliefs and self-love starvation prompted him to take a rather different turn in life and turn to the stock market to compensate for his inner void. Ignoring the signs that his body had subtly presented to him throughout his twenties and thirties, he had in recent years developed more serious conditions that he unfortunately put down as age related. As fate had it, once his new boss decided to demote him, his entire health began to go south—from daily colds to chronic mouth ulcers, poor Max did not seem to be able to catch a break. He had by then not hit the gym in weeks, so his self-esteem and worth had taken a further plunge, leaving the poor sod feeling like he was hitting rock bottom.

Look closer—the answers are inside
of you.

9

Wait... is that a flying unicorn? Distractions and freedom

Once your mind becomes absolutely still, your intelligence transcends human limitations.
~ Jaggi Vasudev

Compensating for hurt

Most people who live outside of inner-self context spend a considerable amount of time chasing their freedom of expression by listening to the nudge of their corrupted egos. They strive for independence but get stuck on the rat wheel of what is accepted and even revered by the world around them. They believe that working themselves to the ground, in a job they deep down care little about apart from the money and the potential social recognition, will eventually present them with the freedom they so desperately seek. The reality is that the more we anchor ourselves in the immediate happiness of what society deems auspicious (such as getting a huge mortgage, a sportscar on finance, the holidays on the credit card) the further away we get from being free. Most often than not, these actions are taken to distract ourselves from our inner turmoil, another form of compensation, and unfortunately there is little freedom in that, if any. We become the inmates of our own-made prison without even realizing it, and still blame someone else for having thrown out the keys when the door gets stuck.

Distracting ourselves by creating endless to-do lists, projects and ventures can also be linked to this call for awareness not being answered. So next time you dedicate yourself to a new kitchen redecoration, plan to have another baby because you feel that your life is a little empty, get married because a year of planning rehearsal dinners would give you something to do, remember to ask yourself whether you are doing all of that because you have a true heart's desire, or because you are looking to fill a void.

Compensating, whether deliberately or unconsciously (by being a workaholic, alcoholic, fitness-aholic, foodaholic, anything-aholic), will always have some roots in hurt, just like addiction. We may tell ourselves that we couldn't possibly function without the four glasses of wine, Coca-Colas or compulsory sets of daily push-ups, but in reality all that we shove into our existence based on the ego representation of the Self is nothing more than the constraints of our minds to comprehend the true source of our inner joy. Ego loves that you're compensating, because atoning without awareness means your focus is not shifted in its direction, therefore allowing it to continue to go on its rampage. The best prevention and cure for addiction or compensation comes in the form of love, by acquiring more self-awareness and finding the guts to ask why you are looking for a hug in a cup. The true opposite of addiction and compensation is therefore connection to our Inner Selves (dare I say, Love? Again??).

Tip: Take a moment for honesty to take center stage in your discussion. What distractions are you imposing onto your Self in order to oppress your fundamental essence? What are you not giving in to? By finding an area of your life to give to without wanting or expecting anything in return (be it energy, time or your wisdom), you allow yourself to help the other person/ cause all while reversing the habit of wanting and desiring. King Arthur was on to something when he said that, *"In serving each other we are free."*

The corner of Max: Max's Inner Self was dancing the conga to get his attention, displaying amazing skills and headstands made to impress, yet Max would not even glance in its

direction. The crazier the dance became the more pain and hurt Max would feel, so his clever little ego came up with a variety of innovative ideas to keep Max's mind occupied as denial worked its magic. From drawing up a new health regime to rearranging the garden shed and the art collection in his study, the distractions were always plentiful and within easy reach. The family's planner was booked for months in advance, so in between his children's endless competitions and grueling commitments, his poor Inner Self had to conjure up more than just a rain dance variation. To be continued, it said, as it went back to the drawing board.

Still your mind. Your soul's voice
is calling.

10

Personal compass: The voice of your heart

The time is always right to do what is right.
~ Martin Luther King, Jr.

How to follow the voice of your heart—with dream interpretation

You have, at all times, a bespoke compass at your disposal. Day and night, in water or at great altitude, this amazing tool is always wholly functional, and at absolutely no charge to you. Fully incorporated and Swiss reliable, it serves as your personal navigation system even if you've never turned it on once in your life—this little puppy never gets old, even if you do.

So why is it that the vast majority of people have never made use of it? The answer is pretty simple: they don't know they have it. In this day and age, there is a widespread habit of subconsciously filing our compass (better known as the voice of our hearts) in a soundproof box in the back of our toolshed and out of our conscious sight. Here, muted and isolated, it has little chance to be heard against the shouting of the ego mind. Not only is that a disgrace to our poor hearts, the sheer waste of resource is gargantuan and quite frankly preposterous given that most people would pay dear money for such an immaculate power.

And since the heart is the intuitive receiver of the messages of our Inner Self, it comes as no surprise that many people live their lives outside of their own inner context, desperately reaching from one safety buoy to the next in the search for land. Luckily the time has now come for a massive liberation effort to free our hearts and steer the boat in the right direction, allowing that voice to point due north instead of going in perennial circles.

Your compass is spinning around, ticking and pulsating all in excitement for your new voyage.

Tip: Your heart tries to speak to you throughout the day; however, it is at night, when your ego's defense mechanisms are down, that it is able to pick up a game of charades and steal the floor. So next time you see that flesh-eating monster swinging his axe at you, it may just be trying to tell you something. If you pay close attention, you will see that your dream-state serves as the whiteboard for your heart's basic communication system. From SOS signals to simple daily advice, the diversity of its messages can vary greatly, although all are there to guide you. Everyone dreams; the trick lies in the ability to store these messages in the long-term memory bank so they can be dissected the morning after. By making it a habit to keep a journal and a pen near your bed, you facilitate the notation of your dreams in almost real time. As you progress and hone your interpretation skills, it becomes easier and second nature to wake up at too-early-AM to scribble down the seven giant bunnies that just finished chasing the crap out of you.

The corner of Max: Max's dreams had started to take a more flamboyant turn with his boss making a habit of mutating into a tall red-feathered peacock out to steal all of his money, with Max guarding his wallet but losing all of his teeth in the process. Needless to say, the S.O.S. messages were getting louder and clearer; though in Max's mind, the land of dreams was a place better forgotten. With the voice of his heart locked in a box, the path ahead seemed grainy at best.

Your inner compass will take you home.

11

Yum Yum Yum—What's your diet? Frequencies and the body

The unexamined life is not worth living.
~ Socrates

Frequencies and diets

As the quality of our thoughts influences our bodies and therefore our overall well-being, you can say that our diet is not solely to be classified by the foods that we consume with our mouths daily, but by a broader spectrum of energetic alimentation such as the frequencies of all that surrounds us.

The very energy that forged the matrix of the universe holds in itself the remarkable ability of infinite expression that is achieved via boundless vibrational frequencies, changing, singing at all times in the great symphony of creation. Since vibrational frequencies are an essential role in the making of your own physical reality (such as atoms and molecules), the interconnection between the electrical frequencies of the human body and that of the world around it are interchangeable.

When the resonance of the body is one of health, it will vibrate at a higher frequency and shield lower vibratory energies from entering and affecting it detrimentally. When this becomes lowered due to stress, emotional hurt or thoughts that are inauspicious to your being, the resonance of the lower energies around you will become a match and create a disharmony in the form of illness or disease. Even here the notion of 'like attracts like' comes into effect. So what you are drawing into your life at any given moment will affect you on a 360° angle.

What we allow into our reality, from music, thoughts, colors, types of communication and language, to the TV channels that we choose to watch, has an impact on our frequency. This includes the company that we keep, the places that we frequent and the things that we do for a living and how we go about it, whether we stress on our way to work every morning or allow ourselves to slow down and listen to the subtler messages of our bodies. This isn't to say that we should sever our relationships, quit our jobs and fly to Tibet to do mandalas; but that we should integrate our conscious awareness more granularly into our daily lives and recognize that our frequencies are always organically present.

Many people gravitate towards a compulsive weekly dose of violence/pain/fear as they are programmed into believing that this is needed in order to be happy. Their environment serves this to them on a platter, readily turning part of their vibrational nutrition into one of low energy; a pattern that if followed on a frequent basis locks them into a state of need and addiction to self-inflicted pain, much like a drug. This is a destructive relationship between the mind-body that can only be identified if there is awareness; when this connection isn't present, we begin to compensate for our emotional pain and transmute it into the need for something external to provide us with what we are inwardly missing.

Alleviating our suffering by reaching for immediate resolution is nothing more than a quick fix. Respect yourself for the beautiful being that you are. Listen to your light.

Tip: Meditation is the holy grail of frequency boosters, and if practiced daily, it can help increase the vibrational rate of your energy. Sense how you feel energetically after a scheduled week of daily meditations: do you feel that you have better mental clarity and therefore better alignment of your higher self? Also remember that the frequency of the people that you hang out with affects your own frequency, so a good question would be whether they are contributing to your positive expansion, or do they have zero nutritional value. Or worse, do they deplete you of your vital energy altogether?

The corner of Max: Max had started to become aware that the customary weekly trip to the movies always seemed to center around violent and aggressive films. The same was true for the television shows that he watched and the music that he listened to. Most of his colleagues and friends had chosen to live their lives inundated with hidden alcohol consumption and subtle negativity, and although Max was on the same bandwagon, he had started to feel incomplete and unsatisfied by the same routines. He felt heavy-hearted after spending his Sunday afternoons with his golf pals and knew that there had to be a correlation between his surroundings and how he felt inside, although he wasn't yet sure what to do about it.

From the menu of life, choose love.

12

Down, down the rabbit hole we go: Breakdowns

Fall seven times, stand up eight.
~ Chinese proverb

Overcoming breakdowns and what they are

Max actually reached out to me a few years ago. He called me in the middle of the night sounding beside himself, sobbing and making those odd clogged nasal noises as he tried to breathe and talk at the same time.

Anyway, here he was, Max Hannigan, 40-something-year-old on the brink of a huge depression, as they usually happen after a lifetime of Inner Self avoidance. After a solid 20-minute monologue, he stopped and sniveled a couple of times: "What do you say? Am I going to die? This is it for me, isn't it? I had a good run, I suppose." I didn't reply immediately. I left a long dramatic pause in the air allowing him to really tune in to what I was about to say. Then in my Shakespearean seriousness I simply said: "Max... I've known you all your life... and honestly... I've never been happier for you than I am right now. F*cking finally!"

He hung up on me.

Don't get me wrong, I wasn't glad that he was suffering of course, but I was happy he finally hit the bottom. In fact, I hope for you too that you will be able to reach the moist ground only to jump up higher than ever before. When you start to experience anger, fear and sadness, you are essentially experiencing the state of separation where you don't yet comprehend or feel that you are part of something bigger than your ego identification.

A key ingredient to most kinds of human suffering is the sharp decrease of control of the ego while experiencing pain.

Most human loss has a similar effect in that it aids you in the fall of the illusory image of your Self that you have held in your mind, the *you* that your ego taught you to identify with. Pain forces you to draw the curtain behind this automatic identification and to become conscious and aware of who you are regardless. Some would say that this is an opportunity for the death of ego, although the ego needs not to die, but to recognize it isn't the one who calls the shots any longer; there is freedom with an integrated ego, but not one that is the ruler of all.

A breakdown can act as a kind of cleansing, a rebirth of sorts, one that will push all of your buttons till there are no buttons left. One that will strip you almost naked as you stand bare in the Antarctic wind with nothing left but you, your last protective coat and your ego to keep you company. Then you realize that the ego you know is just a giant asshole and you tell him to go stuff himself. And then when you are at almost-breaking point, you realize that the protective coat you had fiercely shielded with your life, growling at people if they came too close to touching it, was just a really smelly and old cape made of fear that needed donating or even recycling a long, long time ago. It was an unnecessary security blanket that, instead of protecting you from the cold, was weighing you down, further into the cold snow.

Now I don't know about you, but emotional hypothermia is not a pretty thing. Deep down we're all after that imaginary paradise beach that is always looming on the horizon. And we can all get there; serene and happy we could thrive with coconut drinks and balmy sunsets. But delusionally, we trick ourselves into believing that we are good in the snow with our protective coat; after all we've had this coat for a really long, long time. Why change now? The grass is always greener on the other side, right? Well no, not really, that's just what most have learned to tell themselves when they were convinced that they should settle for less than a blissful life. That's what Max did. That's what most people do.

But you are warriors and a warrior acknowledges his fear and still chooses to go further into the abyss of the unknown. There is a reason for why you feel downcast, don't dismiss it. Contrary to the *'happy-happy let's not go there'* mentality of today, refrain from making yourself feel better momentarily with a round of Candy Crush—dig deeper, you are close.

Tip: Think back to a time where you felt lost and hurt. What identification did you have with your ego mind with regards to what had just happened? What did the moment endeavor to show you?

The corner of Max: Gruesome monthly targets and increasing stress had turned his seemingly great job into a living nightmare. Coupled with the biweekly colds he seemed to attract, staying positive had begun to seem like an impossible task. He half-considered taking to the bottle as his old man had done, but that was just too Loserville even for Max. Then one Tuesday morning when things couldn't have seemed blacker, his boss fired him—just like that. Panic, anxiety and paramount fear did assail him like trained assassins, although there was no denying that a teeny itsy-bitsy part of him felt the smallest of relief. With apathetic eyes and a runny nose, he took an almost-empty train back to suburbia in the hope of disappearing to a faraway land in the process.

Coping well in headwind situations
encapsulates the awareness of every
challenge to be an opportunity
in disguise.

13

Now? Now? What about now? The virtue of patience

Patience is bitter, but its fruit is sweet.

~ Aristotle

Patience

Once we acquire the realization that we are the grand architect of our lives, it's easy to push ourselves harder and become frustrated when things do not appear to be shifting as quickly as we would have liked. We may not consciously identify the reason behind a lingering moment, but the time that our minds perceive as wasted has in fact a tremendous importance in the overall creation of our reality. Energy always works in the background of your stage even when it isn't apparent, so next time that you fall into the pit of undervaluing the importance of every minute of your existence, you effectively dismiss the grandeur of your power—you allow the restricted view of your mind to dictate the order of the day even though it does not possess the capacity to see full circle.

In today's world, instant gratification plays a big role in the foul game of scarcity, a sport dear Ego is a die-hard fan of. Lasting for a mere moment, the quick fixes will give ego the candy that it craves and make sure that it keeps coming back for more, even if that means making you exit your road every five minutes.

Luckily, there is a way to put a stop to that. As soon as you consciously choose to grant yourself the gift of trust (*in* yourself), you welcome patience into the picture. Patience is an admirable ally to have, for not only does it aid in keeping you balanced and grounded on your path, it also prods you into a more relaxed and less needy state of being where you are able to fully attend to the present moment. And since the now is the only place your thoughts should be, patience becomes the headteacher of your mind, lovingly steering it to see what it has in front of its eyes.

Remember that every second counts—trust your Inner Self as you steer beyond the nebulous alleys of your mind.

Tip: Next time you feel impatient about a specific scenario or outcome, pause for a second and trust that your Inner Self is not sleeping it off on some lousy park bench, but is working round the clock on things you consciously aren't aware of. Show it the patience it deserves.

The corner of Max: Max had spent many weeks covered in a thick duvet of self-pity and hurt, growing more frustrated and angry as time unfolded. The pile of rejected job applications made him curl into complete mental stagnation—nothing seemed to shift in either direction. Grave impatience kept knocking on the door, making Max feel like he was about to lose control. But unbeknownst to him, that was exactly what his Inner Self wanted him to do: to stop resisting and finally let go. Luckily Max finally got the memo, and not a moment too soon. He had developed peculiar skin rashes and high fevers which in turn had stripped every ounce of life left from his ego mind, forcing him to surrender completely to the experience. In his darkest hour, kneeling on the ground as he begged for mercy, he finally found the courage to pick his Inner Self up in a fluffy blanket and ask for its forgiveness. His Inner Self was ever-radiant, full of life and embodied everlasting love— it was so happy and exhilarated at finally being brought home.

Every moment of your creation has its meaning.

14

You are not your abilities: Self worth

Low self-esteem is like driving through life with your hand brake on.
~ Maxwell Maltz

Self worth

When people identify themselves with their skills, their worth becomes entirely connected to what they do, and no longer with whom they are innately. This direct identification with the ego mind often leads to hurt and disappointment, because in order to feel accepted and good about themselves, ego makes them believe that they need to do something in order to be worthy of it first—it effectively pushes them to search for a feeling of fulfillment within the identification of their skill sets.

This makes the individual somewhat reject his true self, because even though time and effort spent in an area can help to develop a form of expression, the true self is not in any way, shape or form dependent on its successes or failures to be the light that it is at all times—there is no cause and reaction for the splendor of your Inner Self, it just *is*. When you feel as if you are failing at the game of life, you are actually being given the opportunity to draw the curtains around the illusion of who you think you are and give up on the game itself so that you can experience the unconditional—the so-called 'losing' allows you to remember your natural state and walk away from the need to win in order to feel what you are at all times.

The experience of life within a person is unconditional and it has nothing to do with the external reality that one chooses to lead, so next time ego decides to play his sleazy game of Who is Who, attempt to dismiss it with your authenticity and let go of the attachment to how things should or shouldn't be in your mind—honor who you are regardless of what the desire to be is.

Tip: By giving up on the feeling of succeeding in the area of your life that is consuming you, you let go of that need and free yourself from its hold, disallowing the feeling to define who you are. By giving up on the need to either lose or win, you show up in the game of life without the mask of your so-called identity and allow yourself to just be.

The corner of Max: After losing his trader job with which he had chosen to completely identify for most of his adult life, Max suddenly felt feelings of uselessness, failure and hurt. His direct ego identification with his work game had mutated into a parasitic abomination eagerly feeding on his hidden pain. When his newfound Inner Self reminded him that he was in fact much more than ego had tricked him into believing, Max allowed himself to give up on the need to win at life and instead simply be who he was all along. It took months of daily meditation sessions to finally make Max feel like he didn't have to earn a place in this world... breathing had been enough.

Skill based success does not equal fulfillment—unwavering bliss will only be found within.

15

Look at the pretty bird: The Power of the present moment

Life can be found only in the present moment.
~ Thich Nhat Hanh

Living in the Now

Not living in the present is often just another coping mechanism of our minds to distract us from how we really feel inside, another form of escapism choreographed by our ego mind. The constant obsession of what is going to happen to us in our future or longingly thinking back at the times we were young and single takes us out of the moment that we are in now and disables us from being the conductor of our reality; we instantly lose awareness of our being. The distraction of thinking ourselves elsewhere makes us miss the point of creation that we solely can acquire in the moment.

Many live their entire lives without being fully committed to the present and do not even notice, but the truth is that there is pain and fear in wanting to escape. There is hurt in being in the now and wishing to be elsewhere, and fear in looking at tomorrow and forgetting that tomorrow is being shaped by how you think and feel today. Looking forward to something that is meant to happen in the future creates expectations that are rooted in your ego and driven by either desire or anxiety; when you become controlled by your expectations, you start living a contingent life that creates pressure and keeps your happiness captive to a future that is not yet defined. Your focus becomes shifted towards the illusion of tomorrow where your well-being is explicated in the context of an envisaged future, thus instantly disempowering you from the you that is the creator of the now.

When you were experiencing anything in your past, you were experiencing it in the Now. In the future, any event in your life will be experienced in the Now as well. So you see, you will always be exclusively in the Now; there is no other real place for you to be. Looking for your identity in your past is no more foolish than staring at the future and asking it for an assurance to be saved.

The irony, however, falls back on the ego, because in the present moment, however large our issues seem to be, there is often no pain to be found. In the present moment, right now, nothing is wrong in your existence except for the thought that there is. Think about this one for a moment. Let's take Max for instance. When he got fired and went home to sulk, in the precise moment he was sitting on his couch with a piña colada bawling his eyes out, nothing was actually wrong, not in that moment anyway. He was not in physical pain, he wasn't hungry or thirsty, or cold. His wife was beside him and they were watching Mrs. Fletcher solving one of her murder cases. What allowed Max to feel pain, however, was the choice to allow his mind to redirect its attention onto something that had already happened in the past, and project fear into the tomorrow, therefore allowing full identification with the ego Self. Since the quality of your present thoughts are the ones that create your future, can you guess for how long Max was out of a job?

Tip: Applying the elastic Balloon of Now. The Balloon of Now is a visualization tool to keep your mind focused on the moment at hand. The exact moment you feel your mind start to drift towards a desired situation (the future or the past), imagine a huge restrictive circle of energy encircling your head and pulling it closer to itself, thus minimizing the spillage of your thoughts. Try and do this in conjunction with asking yourself the right questions—there is a reason to why you want to escape from the moment.

The corner of Max: Unemployment turned Max from clean-shaven, dark, tall and handsome to Castaway meets Yeti in the wild. He felt better in nature so most of his days were spent walking in the woods and learning the different names of the many poisonous mushrooms. His Inner Self was guiding him to focus on the little things in front of him, to appreciate the smell of the rain against the bark of the trees and the air in his lungs. Directing his awareness onto the small things of his NOW made him feel centered in who he was, letting Ego sleep his hangover off, and his inner light to awaken slowly from a deep, deep slumber.

Don't wait for tomorrow, the weekend or the next holiday. The future has already started.

16

To believe or not believe, that is the question: The conscious skeptic

Your understanding of your Inner Self holds the meaning of your life.
~ Leo Tolstoy

An open mind

If we could consider spiritual, scientific and philosophical understandings as our fuel towards the fundamental truth of oneness, we would be able to better acknowledge that there is nothing paranormal in the universe except for the currently limited understanding of nature—what man thinks to know on earth is just a teeny tiny drop in the ocean of knowledge.

The ability to keep an open mind about our nature is a prerequisite to conscious expansion, although the whole affair can get rather convoluted if we are expected to hold opinions on every matter we encounter. Whether we are coaxed to be against or for an argument, be believers or nonbelievers, we are habitually summoned by our exterior reality to choose one side of a fence. When there's so much out there for us to process daily, it becomes easier and less frightening to pull blanket decisions and call it a day. Unfortunately, without individual scrutiny we risk falling into the close-minded wardrobe where torpid thoughts and stuffy air become the invisible plateaus on our journey. Ego loves it in there—with no adversary to challenge his steady inflation, the nurture of his illusionary existence becomes effortless.

By turning close-mindedness (fear of change and the seeming lack of control) into skepticism, we cast personal fear of the unknown aside and allow acumen into the equation—we give a chance to what could be based on the open curiosity of our being but tread cautiously on new ground. In a world with no assurances, healthy skepticism becomes our faithful protector. I say healthy, because in light of demanding to see supporting facts and evidence for a claim, the conscious skeptic knows that for a spiritual truth to slot into place, the mind must first connect with the heart—the quest to reach tangible spiritual and self-development evidence is one that is bestowed unto the individual only.

As we let our hearts speak louder and clearer, we allow the intellectual game to be paused for a moment and intuition to unfold at last.

Tip: Next time you hear an idea new to you, pause for a moment and disengage your mind for a moment before introducing it to the conversation that you have initiated with your Inner Self. Could it be that you are rooting for either extremes in order not to lose the illusionary control that your ego mind wants you to have at all times?

The corner of Max: Max had always been the guy who'd have something to say about every subject at any given time. Expert or not, he always had the answer to everything, even if it meant closing the door to learning opportunities. Once his Ego had gotten smaller, this need followed suit, making Max less prone to polemical tendencies and alpha male compulsions. He also noticed that much of what he'd held false or true in his mind no longer felt right to his Inner being, prompting him to connect deeper to his heart for the assurance he had so long hankered for.

Heart knows more than mind.

17

BFGL: The big feel good list

Showing gratitude is one of the simplest yet most powerful things humans can do for each other.
~ Randy Pausch

Writing feel good lists

By understanding the importance of bringing our awareness into the present moment, we train our minds to be grateful for what we experience and have in our lives right now. When you feel as if life is slapping you in the face again, pause for a minute and draw a list of all the good things that you are grateful for; this can be as trivial as seeing beautiful flowers on your way to work, or the smell of those freshly baked baguettes.

The main scope of this is to shift your focus on what you do have and feel gratitude towards it, that way letting the feeling of abundance enter your energy and allowing yourself to finally turn water into wine, because an abundant mindset makes for an abundant life; so the more you train your mind to look for the good bits, the easier you will transform your reality into the land of plenty. You can start with the small things that you take for granted and that you would instantly miss if not there. The things you cherish and enjoy but that you shrug away for being perhaps too mundane to even mention, like the smell of fresh air, the sound of birdsong, the herb patch in the back of your garden, or a beautiful image on the side of the taxi. The feel good list holds all of the things that you enjoy doing, looking at, experiencing and having in your lives, regardless of what they are (though, if I were you I wouldn't put 'having a smoke' on there, but hey that's just me). Call it a pick-me-up list to help raise your vibration and feel uplifted in grander ways than any tonic could ever do.

Tip: So grab that piece of paper, diary, toilet roll or the memo app on your phone, and start writing all of the marvelous wonders that are around you; the richness you attract will come back at you manifold.

The corner of Max: On a rainy and grey Tuesday afternoon, Max decided to whip out his new diary and write his own feel good list. He felt the excitement of a little boy, allowing his imagination to wander to the forgotten corners of his mind, enabling all the beauty that had been dormant to resurface for him to admire. He started by writing the names of his children, adding all the activities he enjoyed doing with them the most, from swimming to baking cinnamon swirls. Then he included the titles of his favorite films, foods, songs and colors. He didn't stop there though, and went as far as listing all the things his body had enjoyed that day, from having a nice warm shower to the soothing feeling of the aftershave on his cheeks. He felt that the more he focused on all the positive bits, the richer he felt in all areas of his life. How priceless. Literally.

Bliss is closer than you think.

18

You are not in *Othello*: The Power of laughter

The human race has one really effective weapon, and that is laughter.
~ Mark Twain

Laughing is medicine

The power of laughter has been documented for its healing powers over and over through the ages of time (thank you, Patch Adams), and for good reasons. There is tangible evidence to highlight the benefits of a good belly laugh, and that the more we do it, the lighter we feel and the easier we're able to move forward and out of strenuous situations. We recognize the importance to seek the chance to laugh more in our lives, to invite the opportunity with open arms and to identify the funny moments despite all the drama that our ego often leaves us stranded in.

When it comes to a lot of the spiritual content out there, the concept of humor seems to be pulling a Houdini from under our eyes. There is a sanctimonious air to the whole quest of knowing oneself that seems to make the spiritual path heavy with misplaced seriousness. Our essence is jovial spirited; it wants to play, experience and create. Seeing the bigger picture, it views life for the theatre play that it is and does not dwell on the small stuff too much. After all, this moment of your life is but a tiny slice of meringue cake that will be gone in a fragment. And although being human entails a slightly different point of view, we would do well in endeavoring not to be weighed down by what our serious minds try to sell us, especially if fear is still the king ruler of our game. We are not talking about denial here, but the realization that no matter how awful a situation may be, you will be able to pull through it—laughter will help you on your way.

When taken too seriously, many situations seem unconquerable and frankly too overwhelming to tackle; but if you are able to laugh at these scary moments before actually dealing with them, the laughter itself will make them seem easier to overcome and less daunting. Laughter and stress are not able to exist in the body simultaneously, so in a way you can say that not only is laughter healthy, it quite literally defeats stress. It is lethal. Don't underestimate Mr. Laughter anymore; under his red nose and multicolored wig, there is a skilled Jason Bourne in action. Next time you find yourself in a pickle, remember to enlist his help, because the best thing that you can do in the lingering difficult times is to acknowledge where you are, however stagnant you may feel in the moment, and find a way to laugh: laugh at the small stuff while engaging in exceptionally trying situations, laugh in the face of fear, laugh at how comical it was to get your skirt stuck up in your underwear at that job interview and trust that everything happens for a reason. Bring back the humor into your lives—laughing is infectious, it's oxygen, it's medicine.

Tip: When we take ourselves too seriously we are often unable to see the bigger picture. Next time you are faced with a challenging scenario, endeavor to take a bird's eye view of your situation and dismiss the ego's need for drama. In the moment, there is often a chance to crack a smile or for even a small chuckle; allow yourself to give into the lightness of your heart.

The corner of Max: Max had been a serious man. Laughing had usually been at the expense of someone else or when he had earned more money than expected. But when life itself had put on a clown face, Max began appreciating the irony that had till then been completely lost on him. He started to see the funny moments for what they were and how they were essential in

getting through his crisis. When he had been wallowing in self-misery, he accidentally caught himself laughing at his own reflection in the mirror. It wasn't *at* himself, it was with himself, with love. He felt his ego getting smaller and smaller, and in its place unconditional love had started to swoop in. With him at the steering wheel, laughing became second nature.

Don't let your ego take itself too seriously—your soul is jovial.

19

Let go of the blankie: Change is the new order of the day

Change is the only constant in life.
~ Heraclitus

The essentiality of change

Unless the notion of change was to have its repercussions guaranteed in the form of pennies from heaven, many people would rather risk contracting a serious case of the hives than go through the motions of a new dawn. It's a common phobia born out of fear, the famous self-made leash of constraint that takes us backwards and further away from our boundless potentialities. It creates an irrational apprehension of the unknown while turning us narrow-minded for the possibilities of what could be, substantially stagnating our development.

As it is, one of the main ingredients for personal development is in fact being open to change and the ability to let go of that fear, to release the nervous hold on the handrail and move independently from the ego. Ego is not a major fan of change for in variation there is uncertainty, odds that it does not like to dabble in too much. He is the abiding supporter of the fixed rules, the ones set in stone and that cement you to where you are; he doesn't care if you want to go places. But evolution requires us to move around, to be fluid with our creations and allow them to take us closer to a non-dual perspective.

The aversion towards change is so strong in most, that any possible transformation is made possible only if absolutely necessary for the overall well-being of the individual. As a situation becomes physically or emotionally unbearable, we are *forced* to take a turn, one we wouldn't otherwise have made unless absolutely compulsory to our self-preservation. When depression looms, we become required to look inward instead of out — as we are pinned to the wall we have no other choice. Trusting these moments as they arise with an open heart and the faith that our Inner Selves know best allows our growth to unfold naturally and without fear, making any necessary change part of our uninhibited expansion.

Tip: When circumstances begin to alter in your reality, instead of inviting the familiar face of fear into your being, try to center your energy towards the soft knowing of your Inner Self by shifting your focus from your mind to your heart. As you meditate and surrender to the wisdom of your being, you will effortlessly begin to feel supported and see the notion of change as the guiding flow of your river.

The corner of Max: Max's friends hadn't called him for more golf. Nor had his colleagues for more happy hours. His acquaintances and some family members had alienated themselves from him completely. For them this new Max persona wasn't somebody they could relate to — he was being suddenly too honest, too deep and too authentic to remain ignorant to his inner truth, and that made them feel uneasy, their egos and their own limited beliefs were steering them well away for their own misplaced self-preservation. Luckily for Max, his tiny butterfly wings had started to emerge from his cocoon and spread confidently into a new beginning. In his natural metamorphosis, Max recognized that going back to larvae life had no longer been an option or a desire — he knew the other butterflies were waiting for him now.

Welcome change as if it were an
old friend.

20

But more, much more than this... you'll do it your way: Discernment

Don't be satisfied with stories, how things have gone with others. Unfold your own myth.
~ Rumi

Trusting your inner voice

Good old Aristotle (and maybe even Frank Sinatra) used to say that knowing yourself is the beginning to all wisdom—I couldn't agree more, yet who do you know in your life that can actually say they truly know their essence? (Not who they have ego-identified with.)

When the voice of our Inner Self is faint, it's easier to lose our way once in a while and become an unceremoniously quick-bite to misleading way-showers that unfortunately do not have our best interest at heart. There are many dogmatic spiritualists who have set their ground rules for how life is meant to be lived according to their beliefs and have no issues branding a sinner if not in full agreement—the message there is that if anyone promises you the Garden of Eden, especially if this garden is not found within yourself, push the red alarm button.

We now live in an era where alternative and esoteric approaches to self-development are becoming more needed and wanted (ergo, business) so it was to no one's surprise when Big Jim and his cousin also found a way to be 'spiritual teachers' and con you for those '12 steps to spiritual bliss' that just don't seem to change your life no matter how many of their workshops you attend. Many lose their will and faith in the whole idea that anything outside mainstream would even be beneficial, but that is why discernment is your weapon of choice here.

Gone are the times of blindly following soothsayers, the gurus, the prophets, a church, any doctrine... the wise ones who allegedly know more than you. They served as anchor points throughout time, provided us with a divine connection when we had none; but that is no longer the objective. We live in an era that is pushing the individual to look within and discern from the masses in order to 'feel, not think' for ourselves what resonates within us: obeying without questioning is no longer in our repertoire. We are here now to become conscious, and for that, dear friend, you need nothing external, only the openness to remember who you truly are.

Tip: When you read/hear/communicate about any form of spiritual content, endeavor to take your time and meditate over it. Your Inner Self already knows what feels right. Use that compass to steer you towards dry land when you get a little too close to the swamps.

The corner of Max: One day Max decided to join *third-eye-r-us.com*, **a carefully crafted 'spiritual' group that promised the meaning of life and instant happiness, something dear Max had started to long for in spades. The promised sacred webinars and special waterfall retreats, sounded like the perfect ticket towards bliss-ville, and for only a fraction of the usual price that week! Unfortunately, as soon as the 4 digit money transfer was made, the online group disappeared into thin air in a quasi magical act. As he rap-cussed himself to sleep that evening, Max learned the very important lesson of always listening to those faint sounding hand bells ringing in the horizon of his Inner Self.**

Don't be afraid to go your own way.

21

Till life do you part: Relationships

If you are brave enough to say goodbye, life will reward you with a new hello.
~ Paulo Coelho

Relationships and vibrations

There are predominantly two types of romantic relationship dynamics in the world nowadays. The first is born out of the wish to unite your essence with the light of another being, thus coming together in some way to form universal love as equal creators. Here, you know that the principle of two halves making a whole restrains you from becoming your own better half so you show up with the self-awareness that you are beautiful and perfect in yourself—you have tended to your inner garden as a meticulous botanist and grown your own seeds for the pretty roses before embarking on the relationship express. A conscious lover, you know how to embody both the divine feminine and the awakened masculine energy and you are aware of how this balance affects the other person. Such types of relationships are rare, because to be able to sincerely and profoundly love another being for who they are (not for how they make you feel), you really need to love yourself unconditionally first and unfortunately that's not highest on most agendas.

Needless to say, the other and more diffused model has a slightly different dynamic in that you are not seeking an equal individual to share your light; you are looking for the light itself, a savior, therefore turning yourself into a martyr. You essentially say to the universe that you are not good enough and that you need someone outside of yourself to bring you your happiness. You create the classic victim-savior dynamic no longer rooted in equality, co-creation and freedom to be, but an unhealthy conjoined twin syndrome that pushes you further into the belief that you need the other person in order to be able to function... you become a slave of your own fears once again. This can also be manifested by your ego mind by finding a person who needs saving, a project—someone that could provide you with a confirmation of self-worth. Many relationships have this modus operandi, though most are completely oblivious to how the whole aggressor/victim cycle is linking them into the chain of enslavement.

And since the ability of unconditional self-love seems to be bestowed onto this rare breed of exotic animals, you can guess that the majority of the seemingly happy couples out there, the ones you have envied when you were single, the ones who maybe even pitied you around the holiday times because you were oh-so-lonely, should really just do themselves a favor and sign up for the next episode of Jerry Springer.

When you decide to share your light and come together with another, make sure to shine at your brightest, be *you* as you have never been you before, and allow your authenticity to unfold and guide you. Your relationships, be they romantic or otherwise, are really just contracts of your Higher selves, arrangements of growth opportunities that are attracted via the appropriate vibration—the higher your frequency, the higher will the ones of the people you attract into your life be. As your vibration goes hand in hand with how you feel and think about yourselves, it is really a no brainer that *'thou shalt love thy selves'* is all you will be thinking about for a while.

Tip: So start by committing to fall utterly in love with yourself. Do that today. Pick up what is holy to you... the Bible, your phone, a picture of your loved ones, anything that is truly meaningful to you. Place your hand on it and I don't know, seal it with the holy specter or something. Then say out loud: *I (your name) vow from this moment onwards to commit to love and respect my being wholly and unconditionally without prejudice and self-criticism.*

The corner of Max: Max had met his wife, Elizabeth, when they were both students. They both liked to shop in high-end boutiques and their three beautiful children all had riding lessons from the age of 3. Range Rovers were parked in the garage, and expensive cruises were the normal family getaways. Yet once Max had started to slowly awaken, he found himself staring back at his wife with slightly bewildered eyes. Who was this person beside him who now resembled little more than just a friend? What had happened to the love he thought they once shared? And even worse, if little Timmy 1, 2 and 3 hadn't been there, would they even still be together? The thought that he could have pulled a dynamic number 2 had suddenly prompted a large lump in his throat to set up camp with a large tipi tent.

You already are in the most important
relationship of your life: Yourself.
Remember to add the sparkle.

22

Connecting the dots: You are the master of your reality

The power to question is the basis of all human progress.
~ Indira Gandhi

Manifesting realities

Every moment that you attract into your life has a divine purpose. You may be relentlessly tired of something you seem to keep inviting involuntarily into your life over and over again, but you fail to recognize that the assumed perpetrator is in fact a messenger of your Inner Self.

We may feel disheartened at the thought of finding love again after having suffered a heartbreak, but in a pattern there is logic, and in that logic there is the message in the bottle that your heart wants you to hear. There is assured salvation within the moment that you abhor, but only if you choose to experience it with awareness. You may want to blame your heart for having led you astray, but it is never your heart that takes you off the path, quite the contrary in fact (beware from where that *want* comes from, ego may make you believe that its hidden agenda hails from your heart when in fact it couldn't be more distant). Hence when you choose the victim card and curse Jack for having cheated on you one last time, try and ask yourself why you would have wanted to attract such a person or situation into your reality in the first place. Then of course go ahead and show him the road and tell him not to come back no more, no more, no more.

Your soul is wise and all knowing. It communicates with you in funny ways when you are not actively listening to it, but trust that it only wants you to find your way back as soon as you can spare it—standing alone on the sideline of creation is not the funniest pastime you can pick out. Empowering yourself with the notion that *yes you can* choose what to experience is by far more entertaining.

To find the answers to the equations of our issues, we must entrust ourselves with the patience and commitment we deserve, because becoming the master of our creation requires us to go through a learning curve like any newly acquired skill. Just like a beginner violinist, we will practice *For He's a Jolly Good Fellow* over and over again until we want to throw up, then we move to the next melody, the next chapter of our self-development repertoire.

Remember that life can stagnate for decades, and it can change in a heartbeat, just like that. It may be frightening to realize we are the true master of our reality, but the earlier we commit to become responsible for all that is happening in our lives, the quicker we can steer the big red bus back onto the bus lane.

Tip: Take a pad and a pen and write down your most pressing issue, the biggest ball-ache that you have in your lives right now. Draw a circle around it and two arrows. One to the left and one to the right. Under the left one list the things that you think are the reasons why the unpleasant situation is unfolding. Here you can blame everyone if you so wish; it's free rein for your mind on that corner of the paper. Then under the right arrow, write what the situation is pushing you to do, the collaterals of what is happening. What are you learning/have learned from the situation? By assuming self-responsibility, what do you feel you need to be more aware of? Then look at the reasons under the left-hand side: could these be a form of escapism from what you already know?

The corner of Max: When Max's wife chose to leave him on a cold October morning, Max had already started to understand

that there was a correlation between what was happening in his external reality and what he was experiencing within. He felt temporarily saddened by what his ego mind had chosen to associate his impending divorce with (failure, fear, alienation, being a bad father, being selfish, a loser... the list was endless), but deep inside of him he knew that although every story has an end, every end bears a new beginning. With only faith left in his heart, he braced himself for some temporary and much-needed downpour before sowing the ground of his new earth.

Everything happens for a reason. And that reason will ultimately always be to steer you back into the path of love.

23

Elementary, my dear: Neuroplasticity and Limited beliefs

The happiness of your life depends upon the quality of your thoughts.
~ Marcus Aurelius

Neuroplasticity and Limited beliefs

Most of us have spent our influential years building neural pathways that have become so automatic we don't even ask ourselves why or when we think the things we do. Our habitual and unconscious thought-patterns have become such an integral part of our immediate reflexes, we're not even aware of them, just like blinking. And as we have discovered earlier, without awareness, we are not able to consciously orchestrate the great symphony of our lives. It all becomes a bit of a circus with weird acts taking center stage occasionally. That's why becoming the Sherlock Holmes of your thoughts is a pretty good idea at this point.

Bring your investigative stance towards the why you think the thoughts you have: are they contributing to your well-being or are they merely stale processes you learned a long time ago? You actively need to take charge of the identification of these automatic thought activities you are not even aware of having and recognize their mechanisms, or otherwise dear Sherlock will end up falling asleep on a train carriage towards the Orient pissed on cheap rosé.

Having a basic comprehension of how your thoughts actually operate can give you a humungous advantage at becoming aware of how your life is behaving. The neuroplasticity of your brain allows you to consciously rewrite how you think and what you think by the grace of your neurons, so the things that you do repeatedly, you become better at; they become an automatic part of you, so to speak. Whereas what you don't make frequent use of is quick to fade away. It is essentially the capability to change your minds out of anything that has been predetermined and develop your human potential by tapping into the conscious awareness.

Limited beliefs are those beliefs that were formed as a type of shield against painful situations, and have at times served their purpose. Their intentions have probably even been good, although most often than not fallacious. They might have kept you away from short-term pain, but where they will lead you is a positive long-term negative one. Most of the limited beliefs that were modeled when you were still children latched onto you into adulthood to create new experiences based on those very same beliefs, thus no longer shielding you, but creating out of false expectations. One of the most notorious examples grounds in money and its power. If you grew up in an economically poor household where you heard your father complain about how badly he had been treated by his wealthy boss, your childhood mind would easily have formed a limited belief that all rich people are bad and that money is an evil power. Without awareness, this connection could have promoted an unhealthy relationship with the energy of money, keeping you in a less than abundant financial position because of it.

The tricky aspect of limited beliefs is that once they are grounded in you, they are sticky and difficult to get rid of, especially so if the rationale behind your belief doesn't connect up with the person that you are today. If it isn't going to make sense to your mind, that belief will stay neatly tucked away in your subconscious mind for the rest of your days. No wonder you have five maxed-out credit cards to buy that sofa.

Tip: The power of asking questions. The answers to most of your questions lie in the *right* questions. It sounds almost too good to be true, but it's a formidable tool that can aid you in uncovering much of what is hidden from your current sight. This is where you safely revert to the 2-year-old you and equip yourself with the famous word that drove your parents insane: *Why*? Why do you feel this or that towards a particular situation? Why do you think you are in the particular scenario that you are in now? Instead of asking why your boss is being such a twat, try something like: what does this situation encapsulate? And what could I learn from it? Why have I attracted my boss into my life in the first place? Since you now know that your internal reality mirrors your external, the answers for both the good and the bad lie in your hands. Peel the onion and uncover the layers one by one; beneath the rage, could there be pain? Or loss? And under that could there be love? Keep going and don't stop asking until you reach the Aha moment. Life really starts to become so much more fun when you realize that you are the creator and not just another Homer Simpson.

The corner of Max: A successful career was something that Max had connected very early on with being accepted. When he was a little boy, his well-meaning father nudged him to study hard, to aim high and enroll in competitive sports. He had traditional 'macho' banters with his dad and got emotionally punished when his school grades were not as good as they could have been. Being a successful businessman, his father saw Max as the prodigious son who would carry on the family name with grace and honor, money and stability, building the empire he himself had only half started. His father's post-war mentality had kept Max enslaved in his own convictions and pushed Max to abandon his Inner Self at the local lost and found corner very early on. Now that he found the courage to look his fears in the eye, Max was no longer sad to see his 110K paycheck go, after all, it was never his heart's true desire.

All you see in your life, is how you feel inside your Self.

24

Cameras are rolling, and action: Authenticity

Knowing others is wisdom, knowing yourself is Enlightenment.
~ Laozi

The importance of being authentic

Some people make an effort to stay under the radar in the hope of not drawing too much attention to themselves by blending into the masses and dimming their own lights completely. They are full of doubts and sculpt their beliefs and personalities around the company that they keep, bartering their authentic selves for the security of being accepted and liked by their families, friends and coworkers all because of their controlling fear of being judged. Authenticity becomes a concept, almost an extravagance and no longer an essential part of being.

The word authentic in itself means 'from the source', the quality of being the real naked you and expressing yourself without encumbrance. It is the You that is comfortable in your own skin, without the mask that many have been accustomed to wear. Being authentic is a courageous act by definition; only a warrior like you could accomplish such a splendid feat.

The peculiar thing is that many of us have inadvertently assumed the idea of playing somebody else in our own life to be okay; that showing one's true and raw essence is a luxury uniquely bestowed upon the monks of the Himalayas or something. This is of course also unanimously believed by everyone around us, thus negating ourselves (our true selves) to become the leading characters of our own movies—we become the supporting acts, the sideline friends, the background nobodies as we waste away the opportunity to take responsibility for our own spiritual well-being.

Being authentic is your birthright, your true essence and your duty not only for yourself but for everybody around you. When you choose to express yourself and live a life centered in your inner truth, you become the light worker, the inspiration, the beacon in the darkness for others to see. Hope, strength and courage is all you will project along your path, and that in itself is more amazing than any PhD you claim to have earned.

Tip: Polish your magnifying glass and channel our dear friend Sherlock once more. Notice when you are being inauthentic in social settings. When do you automatically assume your character's choices and beliefs? Are you sure you even like Prosecco or is it your character telling you that it makes you look cool ordering another round for your colleagues?

The corner of Max: After decades of acting under the light of his fictional Holl-Illusion-Wood, Max was finally being recruited by himself to become the screenwriter of his own life. Here he could have more freedom to call the shots and create the real Max that had wanted to come out all along. He started to witness the narrative flow easier and the story become more congruent, a true award-winning beauty. He donated his golf clubs to the local second-hand center and allowed himself to remember his early interest in breadmaking and marmalade preserves. He felt no shame when he bravely enrolled in an evening course called *The autumn harvest—how to make your jams last longer*. Oh, Phyllis and Ruth were ever so pleased.

Showing vulnerability invites people in. Today speak from your honest and authentic heart.

25

Pilot, neurosurgeon or janitor? Finding your purpose

The meaning of life is to find your gift. The purpose of your life is to give it away.
~ Pablo Picasso

Finding your purpose in life

Just because you are asking yourself what your purpose is after your second divorce, does not mean that you should be feeling like you have none. As long as you have life you have purpose. Your intuition knows what it is that you are here to do; your blueprint in your heart is there. When your heart opens so will the recognition of your purpose, and don't be surprised if it doesn't match up with the expectations of what your ego deems to be an honorable one. If you are thinking and therefore doing things that are in line with your energetic purpose you will feel bliss, regardless of whether your day job is to serve a dozen portions of runny coleslaw.

In Latin the word *spirit* derives its origins from the word *breath,* a nonphysical energy force that guides human beings through their existence by positively linking the body and the individual *stamp of the soul* together through inspiration, so anytime that you are doing something that reconnects you with this idea of spirit (like for example that cross-stitch pillow of Prancer the reindeer) you are being spiritual. This is often the reason behind a person's predisposition towards cooking or working with children or any number of things that make the person feel in line with their true selves.

If you are yet to find what life would like you to do, remember that you haven't been equipped with what you possess for no reason. Your qualities, what you have come to learn, the areas of your specialty (be it to be able to communicate content, be a good listener or really enjoy scrubbing a good floor clean), are all clues to your true purpose, your life's calling. That is not to say that you should be a maid for the rest of your life and be happy about it because you are the Monica Gellar of your group, but more about following the crumbs that your Inner Self has laid out for you. It's an effortless navigation system put in place to guide you to what you came here to do, and all you need here is to follow, pursue your inner voice. It doesn't necessarily have to do with your career or profession—though it might. It's the stockpiled essence of everything you have been, thought, or experienced in your life so far. What you are innately bestowed with, coupled with the experiences you have collected throughout your existence, tells you poignantly of what your journey ahead can be. Your soul's purpose hides in plain sight.

You may at times have felt as if people around you were better at certain things than you, and maybe that was even true. You may not excel in algebra, cooking or being inside an office, no matter how hard you try, but you could yet discover just how incredibly gifted you are at making people laugh or feel great about themselves. Just because you feel less talented than others does not *under any circumstances* mean that you are or ever have been less than anyone else. Regardless of anyone else's judgment, your inner light could not be brighter—always remember that you are beautiful just as you are and refrain from listening to the words of someone else's belief system, and even less to the little sordid voice of your fear-programmed ego. Tell it to go suck an egg while you focus on some R&R time with your Inner Self.

And remember, what you choose to be from today has got nothing to do with yesterday.

Tip: If nobody would know what you did with the rest of your life, what would you do? If you had the life you think that you want, what would tomorrow be like? What from that vision can you actually start doing tomorrow? What change are you afraid to make? What limited beliefs are effectively holding you back? Ask your friends and family what they think you are good at, starting from the small things. Are you the one who always remembers the trivial details that people have told you? Or the one who can uplift people around them by the power of humor? Don't underestimate your quirks, they are what make you YOU, a unique and wonderful being who deserves to wake up in the morning and shine your light.

The corner of Max: As the months passed by, Max had started to feel more connected to his heart and therefore more in tune with his Inner Self. When he was presented with an image of animals in need during one of his meditations, Max initially questioned if becoming a vet could even be an option given his age and background, but as he listed his core skills and aptitudes, it became apparent that becoming Mr. Dolittle was all he ever really wanted. As he signed up for college, he knew that even though ego had been staring defiantly at him with judging eyes, listening to his heart's calling was the only sane option left to take, and more importantly, it was never too late to start again.

What would you do if no one was watching?

26

It's not you, it's me? The Martyr mentality

Self-pity is our worst enemy and if we yield to it, we can never do anything wise in this world.
~ Helen Keller

How not to victimize yourself

The martyr syndrome is just another tactic of the non-integrated ego to make it all about *it* via the victimization of the Self, leaving the afflicted individual with ingrained guilt and more pain. It's a vicious cycle of unworthiness, inauthentic sacrifice and discontentment (that will 9 times out of 10 end in the resentment of not having been praised sufficiently for the misplaced acts of altruism).

This particular complex can only unfold when unconditional love is not an element; when you are starved of self-love to this degree, the ego is forced to think of tactics to try and get the love from somewhere else, and since ego is limited in its imagination, its resources will come in the form of mind games such as emotional manipulation, blackmail and denial. The latter is self-inflicted and allows the martyr to remain unaware of their behavior and effects on others while they go on their self-victimization stampedes, often at the expense of the ones around them.

Here the ego, instead of inflating itself to appear pompous and ferocious, actually curls into a fluffy ball of what *it* thinks is pure cuteness and admirable saint-like traits, although the truth is far from adorable. The apparent selfless demeanor becomes an infiltration technique used to distract their environment and inflict projected guilt and shame for the benefit of some spotlight and appraisal, turning their own lack of self-love into everybody's battle. Since the core belief of the martyr is one of unworthiness (although consciously they may deny this) their entire behavior becomes optimized to seek situations or people to assure them otherwise—but as like attracts like, where they usually end up is in hate-filled scenarios with drama at its very center.

Martyrdom can afflict any individual at any stage of their lives; although if undiagnosed, the syndrome will grow larger and become more entrenched as they grow older, making a lifelong martyr one of the most difficult people to have around. As always, love is the medicine, although being able to see the dynamics in action allows both the martyr and the observer to be fully present in the moment thus making awareness the number 1 weapon.

Tip: You may be the martyr yourself or you may have martyrs in your family or friend circle. Forgiveness here is always key. Find the strength to forgive yourself for not yet being able to love yourself unconditionally, and forgive them for the hurt they may have caused you without knowing the force behind it. Acknowledge the situation for what it is and endeavor not to look the other way. Go deeper into your meditation and allow the little voices you have tried to bury surface into your consciousness.

The corner of Max: Max's mother had always played the martyr role, ever since he was little. Poor mummy was always in need of saving, no matter what the circumstances were. His own dad reveled in the notion of being needed and branded as the hero for saving her days, although Max didn't quite share this vision. Throughout his adulthood, Max and his mother's relationship had become stagnant and detrimental to both, with normal conversations often ending with dear mom feeling neglected and mistreated. Now that Max had met his true self,

he was no longer inviting drama into his life, so when he went to his mother's house for afternoon tea, he decided to speak to her with the honesty of a child and the compassion of Mother Teresa—he held her hand and patted her hair when he told her how he loved her and how he himself had suffered while growing up. He spoke with authenticity and a clear conscience as he invited her in to see the real uncompromised him. His mother cried, as she usually did, but this time her tears were made of a different sort; they were authentic, loving and understanding like they never had been before.

Love yourself the way you want others to.

27

Hercules no more: Perceived strength

Love is not love until love's vulnerable.
~ Theodore Roethke

How to be strong while feeling weak

Being strong-minded has mistakenly been associated with enduring pain. People have become masters at suffering on the inside and feel okay about it.

But emotional strength worth admiring should be associated with being honest with ourselves, transparent, completely at one with how we feel—being strong enough to face our buried fears. Strong to admit that we may feel low at some point and allow ourselves to cry; that's true strength. Most people can get into the denial stage and bite the bullet, but being able to meet that part inside of you that may hurt like hell in the moment and confront it point-blank, that's buff. Not only will it help you stay true to yourself, it will also inspire others to feel okay to open up about their own battles, so it's really a win-win for all.

For some absurd motive, being a strong person is still associated with enduring the tough times without asking why you have brought that particular situation into your life in the first place, and whether you could avoid that particular pain-pattern from entering your life again. Those who are brave enough to walk into the unlit rooms of their minds know the importance of doing some inner spring cleaning once in a while. Because I hate to break it to you, it can get kind of messy in there... your heart is often dusty and full of spider webs in its mouth.

You don't need to suffer in silence anymore. If you hurt it's because something inside of you is trying to get your attention, not because someone or something is out to pull the rug from underneath you. You may believe that all you need to do is to wait until the pain passes, as it eventually did before, and sure, it probably will. But you can also rest assured that that particular Mr. Pain will pull a Terminator and be back, again and again, until you have finally learned whatever lesson you have set yourself out to learn. And unless you are actually INTO pain from a recreational point of you, I'd suggest you take the shortcut and go listen to your big pumping red organ... what have you got to lose?

Tip: During your next meditation, listen to the small signs that both your body and heart are sending you at all times. Are they trying to shift your attention inwards? That pain that you may be holding onto, do you think you still need it in order to be happy?

The corner of Max: Max had never been one to show emotions in public and felt embarrassed by other people's vulnerability. Crying was a weakness and sadness an emotion best left ignored, a motto he had followed rigorously throughout his adult life. But since rock bottom had forced him to formally meet with all his buried sorrows, Max had experienced the releasing power of a good crying session. He had felt the tears spring uncontrollably out of his eyes as years of toxins were released — not only had he been able to process newer pain, he had been dealing with older feelings, the ones he had wished gone for good decades before. In that moment they had all come to visit him from the most remote corners of his being in canoes and catamarans built for the strongest of floods, and were greeted one by one before being set free on the river of his tears once more. It was a clearing process that taught Max never to deny an emotion from being heard ever again, and to embrace them for the wisdom that they held.

Vulnerability is the bridge towards connections.

28

I release me: The Power of Forgiveness

The weak can never forgive. Forgiveness is the attribute of the strong.
~ Mahatma Gandhi

Forgiveness

When feeling victimized (and therefore powerless), it's easy to allow sentiments of bitterness and rancor to barge in without much thought. The unchecked ego revels in these feelings because they serve as the coal to fuel its phony sense of control, allowing the individual to identify himself with the notions of hurt and anger. This tactic creates a neat cushion for the victim-aggressor dynamic where control is assumed to be gained by bestowing guilt onto another being. Although ironically, the only thing it serves to create is a shiny self-made chain of enslavement that is entirely detrimental to the individual experiencing those feelings.

By understanding the correlation between the act of forgiveness and becoming empowered, letting go becomes not only imperative for the nurture of your Inner Self but also one of the most supreme gifts that you can bestow unto your being; it becomes a power of insurmountable importance that has the ability to set you free instantly. By forgiving others and yourself, you allow the flow of love back into your veins, thus meeting that side of you that sees happiness not as your right but as your duty.

A warrior of light knows that he cannot carry feelings of hatred because he is aware of the hurt that hides inside of it. Too heavy and way too repressing, hurt has no place in the backpack of his being.

Tip: Is there a person in your life (this can even be yourself) that you carry resentment towards? Once identified, ask yourself this: By continuing to carry that feeling, do you add quality to your life?

The corner of Max: Max had grown to despise his old man for the hurt that he had caused him, letting the hate consume him when he was at his lowest. The hurt camouflaged itself in black anger which allowed ego to assume aggressive control over his emotions, but little did he know that anger is a heavy trickster. And as Max had started to feel lighter and freer, an anchor that bulky was not going to cut it anymore. Not only did he feel an enormous weight lift off as he forgave his dad, he felt more powerful than he could ever dream to be—the power to realize that he was truly in control of all his emotions and that no one could ever take that from him.

Forgiveness is the key to your heart.

29

Angel disguised as Billy-Joe the Plumber: Synchronicity

Synchronicity is an ever present reality for those who have eyes to see.

~ CG Jung

The power of Synchronicities

So you know when Billy-Joe comes round to fix the kitchen pipes and he starts talking about last night's reality TV... and then he suddenly says something that really jolts something in you? I mean Billy! The school hater who sees books as malignant sources of alien sorcery just made you uncover something in yourself that was imperative for you to remember at that exact moment in your life. In fact, so important that if he hadn't been there to do it, an essential step in your life would not have been made possible.

Or when you bump into your old school friend Steve that you haven't seen in over twenty years (yes, the kid who gave you all of those wedgies) and who out of the blue tells you that he's working for a top ad agency that is currently looking for someone with exactly your skills, just when you were thinking of changing jobs.

Forget coincidences, 'cause there are none; this is the real-life sliding doors, the endless jigsaw of possibilities that we as an interconnected species are able to weave together like a Pennsylvanian quilt effort. The key lies in recognizing these moments for the synchronicities that they are, which from a non-dual perspective represent the oneness that we all are part of at any given time in our lives. Being connected to your inner selves by listening to your intuition (which really is the ability to see with your soul) will allow you to capture the wonders of synchronicity and become aware of the constant support you are being given.

We are all bound in the most wonderful and laborious ways, infinite strands of energy constantly interchanging, weaving, pulling into each other to form reality as you know it. If you could see the amazing chemistry of our labyrinthic connections, you would be truly astounded of just how 'one' we all are with each other.

When you start noticing how your own existence links up with those of others, don't go thank the fairies just yet; first of all thank yourself. Empower yourself with gratitude for your wonderful ability to attract your innermost desires without lifting a finger. Because that is recognizing the endless power that you all possess; even if you are not aware of it, manifestation happens all the time. It is not something that you start doing when your awareness expands or you become conscious of it. You manifest every nanosecond of your entire lives, right now too. You attract or you push things away, it's really that simple.

Tip: Become aware of how your external environment mirrors your internal reality. When you don't feel happy inside, you will undoubtedly manifest nuisance and pain into your existence. Conversely when you feel at peace, you will attract happiness and serenity, even the small stuff in your life just seems to become undemanding. When you are aligned to this blissful state (which is your natural state of being), you start bringing the positive synchronicities into your life because you are a vibrational match to them. You suddenly meet the right people at the right places and just at the right time. You are in sync and even the birds seem to be smiling at you. And remember that synchronicities do not merely belong to the perceived positive moments of your life. When you start experiencing a series of absurdly linked events that just seem to want to throw you off your horse (such as for example losing your job, your girlfriend and your dog in the same week) know that synchronicities are at play.

The corner of Max: On a spring morning, Max found himself in a part of town he had never ventured to before. The heavy rain had forced him to take unexpected shelter in a café just as an old school flame had walked in. As he saw 1993 walk back into his life, he knew that synchronicities were at play and didn't doubt the flow of life ever again. He thanked himself for having been aligned to the meet cute and braced himself for the sweet ride that only synchronicity can provide. From then on, every event and every moment of Max's life was regarded as the canvas for the marvelous creations of his newfound Inner Self.

You are attracting into your life whatever experience is most essential for your evolution.

30

Sim sim salabim! The Law of Attraction

To live is the rarest thing in the world. Most people just exist.
~ Oscar Wilde

The Law of Attraction

So here's a greatly misunderstood topic out there for you, and may I add, the most commercialized of the alternative approaches to self-development.

In a nutshell, the Law of Attraction (or Resonance) is the ability to attract into your lives whatever you focus on. It is not a mysterious conjecture that applies to some selected individuals, nor is it a tin-hat trick made in the New Age cauldron, but a quantum physics law. A law that very much like the one of gravity makes up the underpinning of our lives at all times. Scientific tests have been able to show that the energy we transmit into an object through observation helps select what happens next in the reality we are choosing to experience right now. So when you hear that your thoughts create your reality, this law is the force behind it; you either work with it or against it.

Unfortunately, most of the teachings, workshops and courses that use the Law of Attraction to bring material goods and abundances into your life do not reflect actual spiritual growth messages, and instead feed off your ego minds to push you further into the desire/fear river. Many use false advertisement to fuel the ego by the riches of materialism while using the makeup of ancient truths. They will sell you how to attract the car that you wanted, the girl of your dreams and your job in 10 easy steps. The idea is being sold as unbelievably attractive, although in essence it tells you that you have been a moron for your last 40 years because if you had wanted you could have won the lottery every single year of your life! You are such a dummy! But it's okay because their seminar is going to change your life and you too could stand on an enormous stage with a microphone attached to your designer shirt talking to the elite of society about how they can boost their profit from 10 million to a gazillion… You can have more and more, yes you little greedy suckers.

But the principle of the Law of Resonance works in conjunction with one's soul's agenda and trajectory, which means that you may want something dastardly with your mind, but if that isn't aligned with what your true self wants, the victory will be short-lived and little more than just energetic manipulation, a temporary distraction. And this is only if that desire isn't born out of need, because as 'likes attracts like', neediness pushes your desire further away into a black hole of nothingness, hence the many dissatisfied customers eager to get their money back from the shopkeeper of Resonance. And since ego is one needy little dog, you can guess how few people are actually able to manifest their true hearts' desires.

Once you consciously start listening to your hearts, the Law of Resonance will allow you to manifest your innermost callings from the wisdom and the intelligence of your soul, and that's just a little bit cool.

Tip: When you identify a desire, where does that intention come from? Is it from your ego or your heart? Why do you want what you think that you want? And is it to compensate for a void or is it an expression of your Inner Self? Attracting abundance into your life starts in the moment you allow yourself to think from the land of plenty and cast away the notion of fear under which your ego is comfortably sitting.

The corner of Max: Max had by now started to live a more Spartan life, with less possessions and more integrated

wisdom to provide him with his joy. When two job placements came his way over the span of a single day, he knew that his abundant mindset had been the facilitator. He was aligned to the wants of his Inner Self and was no longer a listener to the neediness of his now better-behaved ego. Swimming with the current of the universe had meant that Max could finally focus on how he felt and therefore endeavor to fine-tune his vibration to its highest so equal vibrational matches could be welcomed with ease.

You are always creating your reality out of fear or out of love.

31

Bliss is only a thought away: The Power of Visualization

You are today where your thoughts have brought you; you will be tomorrow where your thoughts take you.
~ James Allen

Visualization techniques

Placebo effect or not, choosing to believe in what serves you well is not only the cleverest choice in order to attract happiness into your life, it is also the most effortless. Once you cast aside the victimization mindset, you become able to consciously create your reality with your thoughts and mold every step of your path with the light that you choose to cast upon it—you have that power.

By applying visualization techniques into your daily lives, you allow an event/person/dynamic to enter your reality with more ease. Everyone can use their imagination. Though many brand this quality as something childish, a gift no longer useful, a mere fleeting distraction routine at best when they wish to be elsewhere (unless you are a novelist or a children's storyteller, in which case you are allowed by society to keep it with pride). The truth, however, is that in the power of imagination lies a whole universe of abundance ready to be discovered. There hidden in the magnificent power of your creation, real-life superpowers are alive and most have never even glanced in its direction.

Luckily it's never too late. You can call upon this power at any time of the day, wherever and whoever you are—as long as you are breathing this little gem is yours to keep. You know that you are in control of everything that is happening to you, so when you begin to consciously use your creative imagination for the manifestation of your heart's well-being, you not only allow its dreams and goals to become real and tangible, you also align yourself to the trajectory of your Inner Self, and that's when real-life miracles can take place.

Trust that your Inner Self is always taking care of you, have faith that it can, and the courage to let it.

Tip: Next time you take a shower, imagine the water washing not only the dirt away from your body, but your worries, your fears and your anxieties; look at how the water caresses every inch of your being and takes all you no longer need away with it—feel it with your heart as the droplets steal away the negativity you no longer want. As you enter a vehicle, the very moment before allowing the smallest of anxieties to creep in, envision a dome of light encircling you—feel the invisible energy protect you from the corruption of your ego mind and what it is trying to feed you, because in a fearless state, darkness has no backdoor in.

The corner of Max: Max had travelled to many exotic places in his lifetime, from the Maldives to Florida, Paris and Thailand. Although on top of his travel list, there had been a place no one else had wanted to visit with him, making that trip to Vietnam an improbability. Now that he had no one else to listen to, he felt a great pull to travel there; although unfortunately, Max found himself for the first time in his life without much money. Knowing about the power of visualization, he started to imagine himself roaming the streets of Hanoi, down to the details of his shorts and flip-flop design. He would sit during his meditations and pretend that he was purchasing his airplane ticket and accommodation by next fall. And as manifestation has it, a few months later, Max received an unexpected and rather handsome tax return, making that trip of a lifetime suddenly very possible. Spring roll for one please.

Abundance is a state of mind.

32

An abundant life: Gratefulness

Gratitude is a currency that we can mint for ourselves, and spend without fear of bankruptcy.
~ Fred De Witt Van Amburgh

How to invite abundance by the power of gratefulness

When we are unaware of the power of our creation, it isn't easy to attract an abundant state of being into our lives—blaming others has after all been the habitual choice. But in order to get to the other side of the pond where the grass is greener, it's important to realize the power of gratefulness and just what an important role it plays (especially when we feel stuck in second gear).

If we are financially struggling, it's simple to fall into the circle of self-pity and feel the familiar mixture of anxiety and worry creep in as we receive our bills. Blaming politics for the soaring prices and waiting with anguish as more bills hit the fan is easy; though ironically, all it will be conducive to is even less abundance, allowing scarcity to remain the dictator of our life. Since being grateful while experiencing pain doesn't come second nature to most, taking the backdoor in becomes necessary. As you look at your dire bill as it comfortably sits in between your fingertips, it's helpful to remember the benefits the service has provided to you, whatever it might be. If it's electricity think of all the television or radio or computer time it has allowed you to have. Feel grateful in that moment and allow yourself to focus on all the positive aspects of having had the opportunity to do the things you wanted, be it to watch an episode of *Frasier* or making yourself that lovely cup of tea.

And don't stop with the bills. Look at every area of life where a void is felt, be it friends or love, laughter and fulfillment. Most often than not, when you feel something is missing, you will find your gaze shifted in the opposite direction of abundant-town. The good news is that once you are aware, you can consciously look towards greener pastures and effortlessly attract them to you without even having to go there. Score.

Tip: Think of an area in your life where you feel scarcity. This can be anything at all, small or big. As you know that like attracts like, what do you already have in this specific area? If love is what you desperately miss, in what form do you already have love in your life today? If it's your career, what aspects of your current situation are favorable already? Get your pen out and draw a list of all the things that every seemingly lacking area of your life already has. Being grateful for what you already have is the fastest ticket to feeling like a king (or a queen). And that's when synchronicities appear and it all goes ahhhhh.

The corner of Max: Ever since the divorce and the drastic change of life, Max had seen many of his family members drift further away from him. He wasn't particularly sad about seeing his cousins and uncles go in a cloud of fine cigars, after all he had nothing in common with them anymore. But he did grow to miss some family unity, especially around the holidays. He longed to be able to include his children in a more extended family capacity; so as soon as Max identified that desire, he started to meditate over every good thing he currently saw and had in his family. From his kids, to the improved relationship he had formed with his own mother, he focused on all the positive aspects and wrote down a list of them all. Within a short time, he found himself arranging his son's birthday with the help of a long-lost sister, an eccentric auntie he hadn't known very well and a couple of new good friends who had replaced the family members that were no longer in his life.

As the party arrived, he saw himself surrounded with love, laughter and warmth and realized in that moment that being grateful is a power never to be undervalued.

Gratefulness is a magnet for the extraordinary express.

33

Oh, isn't she just modest! Humility in action

All limits are self-imposed.
~ Icarus

Humility vs modesty

It is easy to fall into the pit of false modesty while digging ourselves deeper into the fear mentality of today's world. Masquerading self-deprecation for modesty is nothing but a skewed manipulation attempt by the non-integrated ego to keep you centered in the victimization routine that you have been accustomed to—by relinquishing your self-responsibility as the creator of your reality. When you apply false modesty to your everyday life, you begin to sing an inauthentic tune for everyone to hear, and you forget that the reason for this is really, once again, due to your lack of unconditional self-love. Your Inner Self knows that it is beautiful just as it is and that it holds uncountable little gems of wisdom. You only need to shift your attention towards it to be able to see them, by going inwards.

The word modesty comes from the Latin meaning of 'within measure'. Historically connected to how a person was expected to behave and dress within a society in order to be socially accepted and respected, it has in today's world linked itself more in the virtues of humility and unpretentiousness (though humility is rooted within the internalization of the Self whereas modesty more in the externalization—applied to receive). And while these attributes of humility are the stepping stones towards the antonym of vanity and egotism, it is important to be able to identify when they are being used as a Trojan horse to bring mere disparagement to one's self-worth for the benefit of external acceptance.

Many people are programmed to respond to praise with an automatic and false sense of modesty in order not to appear worthy (even if inauthentic). When somebody admires or congratulates us for something that is well deserved, we often enter this approach to diminish ourselves in the eyes of others, hoping (not consciously) that they would in turn recognize this outwardly admirable (and misinterpreted) quality, and see us for the aspiring martyr that we are—it becomes just another tactic of the ego to become liked and accepted by others. But genuine humility is rooted in the authenticity of your expression and the awareness of not letting your ego dictate the order of your day—by being yourself and good at what you do without the *expectation* of praise. When and if you then get lauded, you will receive it with gratitude, allowing yourself to feel worthy and acknowledge that you did a good job (perhaps even thanking the people that were essential for your accomplishment).

Being able to accept a compliment becomes natural and even inspiring for others since what you are expressing is sincere and from your heart, helping them to believe that they too could excel by being true to themselves. Once you are able to love yourself enough and not care if others are going to pat you on the shoulder when you have finished the PowerPoint presentation that you were up all night doing, you will be able to appreciate that all that you are longing for is already inside of you (yes, yes it is love, you guessed it).

Tip: Next time someone gives you a compliment, look closely at your reaction. Are you able to accept it or do you automatically dismiss it?

The corner of Max: Once Max had started to volunteer at the local cat and dog shelter, he began to receive many compliments for his ability to connect with the animals. People around

him would notice his nurturing side and admire his aptness for forming instant bonds. In the face of compliments, Max learned to receive with gratitude, which not only became an extension of his self-love and respect, it also inspired younger apprentices on site to believe in their own abilities.

Recognize your inner light even if you cannot see it.

34

To be a visionary means to be misunderstood: Living a life from the stamp of your soul

What we achieve inwardly will change outer reality.
~ Plutarch

Life from the Inner Self

Once you have acquired a certain sense of self-awareness, you will undoubtedly start feeling like a sheep who has lost its way a little. You will look back at the pack and wonder why none of the others are willing to join you. You may feel disheartened by the wish of many of your friends to remain grounded in a fear/pain reality. You may feel lost and alone, because once your ego no longer rules all, the common pastimes of your friends may seem silly, inconclusive and out of context—drowning your sorrows by doing a pub-crawl will probably not appeal that much to you anymore.

There may come a time when you will think of clocking out because feeling alone and like an alien in a Middle Age civilization will test your limits, but that's when you will have to walk an additional mile and understand the prodigious value of actively participating in your life by being conscious and aware. Though no one is going to congratulate you for it or even acknowledge your bravery for having climbed your mountain, refrain from isolating yourself for the rest of your life in order to experience that bliss you have finally found. That bliss is yours, you have earned it, no one is ever going to take it from you, but as *Spiderman* so eloquently put it, with great powers come great responsibilities, and with all that wealth of love that you now possess for yourself, you will be able to *consciously* live life from within the masses, and that will change everything.

Participating in the game of life with your highest state of awareness is the biggest gift you can bestow onto humanity. You don't need to write a best-seller or go to Africa to become a spiritual missionary; *being* aware is all you need to *do* and will count so much more than anything you can conjure up in your mind. It's not about the status or stature of what you do in your life, but the degree to which you are connected to your inner light and organically become that light of energy for others. You can't check-out and be as effective—participating in the world and knowing that it is all an illusion will allow you to play it from a heightened state of awareness. Imagine how the self-aware taxi driver can drive through Manhattan and take his inner light consciously through the streets for others to vibrationally feel. He would change the whole damn town by just being. He would inspire, ignite and affect more lives than you can possibly imagine.

So carry on bringing the stamp of your soul into your awakened consciousness, merge the DNA of your spirit into who you are and go about living your daily life from this heightened state of being. You are changing the world and saving lives as we speak. Cue the gospel and hallelujah.

Tip: If you feel a little out of place and disconnected from the rest, try to take a moment to realign yourself with your core energy. There is a reason for you to be here right now; allow your Inner Self to show you what that is. By focusing more on your own well-being and on the expansion of your light you help everyone around you in ways you or they could never have imagined. Imagine your soul moments before your birth—envision its enthusiasm of going on its trip on earth. In its pre-journey excitement it would have packed maps, compass and Inner strength. It would have been impatient the night before as it eagerly anticipated its trip. You are that trip, the enthusiasm and that excitement all at once—remember how far you've come to be here now and enjoy it while it lasts.

The corner of Max: Sometimes Max couldn't help but feel disconnected from his surroundings. He felt misunderstood and at times downcast at the thought of having to live life with people around him that did not always share his newfound awareness. Then one winter's night, when nothing seemed to have shifted for many months, he realized that by just being himself he was fulfilling any purpose he could ever have had. By being centered in himself, by being honest and authentic and keeping his own vibration at its highest, he was lighting everything up around him, even if people didn't consciously recognize it, on some level they did. And that realization made everything in contrast seem more worthwhile.

Carry on your path and bring the stamp of your soul into your life.

35

Ooga chaka, ooga ooga chaka…: Using affirmations to uncover repression

Most powerful is he who has himself in his own power.
~ Seneca

How to use affirmations in your everyday life

Repressing the existence of an undesirable feeling will not automatically cause it to disappear, so placing the deconstruction of the self-hate identification in the top 5 things to do before embarking on the affirmation boat is a pretty good idea, as obstructing any such feeling from surfacing will only amplify their roots as they continue to hide from your ego sight (and just because you can't see them doesn't mean they are not there).

Mantras and affirmations can serve as powerful tools to boost your vibrational energy, and if used in conjunction with the absolute awareness of how they affect your resonance, they allow you to connect your mind to something larger than your life. If you notice any type of resistance towards the words, pause and ask yourself where that limited belief comes from, how it was formed—by going back to its source, you are able to easily identify it and say farewell to it.

Be meticulous in the way that you create your personal affirmations, as every word and sound contain their own unique set of energy, so if the frequency of a specific word does not flow easily in your being, change it for one that does. The words of God/Almighty/Christ are for example often linked to something both anachronistic and not relatable, so if it doesn't resonate with you, change it. You are, as usual, the creator here; don't follow the criteria of others, follow yourself.

Tip: Here are some ideas to get you started with your affirmations.

I am surrounded by love
I feel innate worthiness
Today is another day of limitless possibilities
I open the door to abundance
I believe in myself
I make myself proud
I forgive myself and allow myself to become free
I let go of what no longer serves me good
I feel supported and loved
I honor who I am
I am courageous
I walk in the light
I am healing all my hurt with every breath that I take
I am unique and special
I radiate love and happiness
I embrace the rhythms of my life
I am the architect of my reality
I can (*insert here what you would like to become better at*)
I AM worthy of (*insert here what you would like to attract*)

The corner of Max: Max had found that by creating his own daily affirmations, he was able to feel more in touch with his Inner Self and hit any goal that he set out to achieve, from attracting a new lady companion to meeting like-minded friends and be the dad his children deserved. Affirmations empowered him from within his core and enabled him to express himself in a grounded and more authentic way. Not even the sky was the limit for how fantastic these could be.

Love yourself for you are splendid,
worthy and so needed.

36

Got money? Aligning yourself with the energy of money

Wealth flows from energy and ideas.
~ William Feather

The spirit of Money

In the world of today, money has become an essential energy-form that either flows into your lives or is met at your door with some subconscious resistance. When those limited beliefs are rooted in a strong financial aversion, chances that the gateway of economical wealth is going to shut in your face are pretty favorable.

As it stands, money has often been linked to negativity, the root of evil, what is corrupt and all that derives from the greediness of human beings for wanting more and more in an increasingly materialistic-driven society. Very often, when people begin their soul journey, money becomes a major aspect of what used to represent their self-identification prior to embarking on their trip to their inner light, making it something of less value or even disliked. They throw it aside in the belief (firmly backed by their spiritual ego) that in order to be spiritual minded/a light worker/a healer/someone with good or valuable traits, one must follow the trail of what is being represented as holy/good and rid oneself of all that possesses financial energy in order to embody that spiritual purity. And while there is a valid point in wanting to live a simpler life fueled by the soul and values that root in non-possessions, the importance of recognizing your current life-cycle and the timeline that you have chosen to live in will make the acceptance of money being a mere energetic instrument of use to all that live among it easier and more transparent. When we begin to view money as sheer energy, we'll be able to observe *how* this energy is behaving around us and intuitively begin to feel how its subtle form is either a welcome part of our lives or a mosquito inside our net—the choice is of course always ours.

Whatever the reason behind the friction, being able to reconnect with the spirit of money can aid you in the creation of your spiritual life while being consciously aware of how you are playing it. It becomes your ally, your friend, your ever-present gizmo at hand in your tool belt.

Tip: A good exercise to introduce money back into your life is to take a bank note and put it in between your hands. As part of your daily meditation, try to set a few minutes aside to just sit with the note in your hands and feel the warmth of it in your palms; become aware of its energy. Introduce yourself as if you were meeting a new acquaintance and wait for its reply. Don't rush this process; let any image that wants to surface take center stage here—you want to identify any sources of limited beliefs by going back to where they all started, allowing your inner voice to talk. You may see yourself as a child being conditioned by someone else's belief, or witness a negative effect of the mistreatment of money. Whatever it may be, invite it in, observe it. Then once you are ready, thank it with your heart and say goodbye to it, release it, you no longer need it. You may repeat this exercise a few times as there may be several blocks impeding you to allow money to even reach your frequency, so have patience and persevere. Once all blocks have been eradicated from your subconscious mind, allow the energy of the money (the one that you are still holding in your hands) to enter your own energy field, to feel it in your body and your mind; let it merge with them. You can envision this by painting the energy of money with a color of your choice, brushing it with a rich pigment and allowing it to fuse with you—feel the aliveness of it add vitality to your being. It will enrich you from an integrated perspective and allow you to express yourself with the full awareness of energetic fluidity.

The corner of Max: Max was happier than he had ever been. His life was prospering in all areas and he was able to feel love in ways he hadn't thought possible. Once he was able to rid himself of limited beliefs that had dictated his old life, he was careful not to write up new ones that were in any way detrimental, so as soon as he saw how he had antagonistically treated money in the past year, he recognized a pattern ready to be broken. He went to the nearest ATM and withdrew a $20 bill. After meditating with the energy of money daily for weeks on end, he was finally ready to let go of past patterns and welcome it back into his life. Money was happy to come back because, as it happened, it had been knocking on Max's door for quite some time.

By letting go of fear you allow abundance
back into your reality.

37

Was that a yes, a no or just maybe? Fine-tuning Intuition

The intuitive mind is a sacred gift and the rational mind a faithful servant. We have created a society that honors the servant and has forgotten the gift.
~ Albert Einstein

How to tune into the power of intuition

Intuition is the subtle knowing of something without concrete reasoning. It's the gut feeling that takes you to the places you wouldn't have visited had you purely relied on the counseling of your mind.

Unfortunately, the cultural bias against following our intuition often leads us to disregard our perceptivity and ignore altogether the little invisible hand that steers us towards more opportune choices. Many tune considerably more into the whole anxiety/fear energy combination so that their alert bells are almost solely receptive towards imminent threat (such as terrorism, end-of-day viruses, and rapacious individuals out to steal our purses). With the focus permanently fixed on the eye of Sauron, it's nearly impossible to pick up any nudge from the heart, and that's a pity.

As we learn to acknowledge the importance of being open to change, we acquire the flexibility to follow our intuition wherever it may want to lead us, meaning that we aren't going to oppose too greatly when cancelling our next mani-pedi appointment just because we feel an unexplained pull to do so—we may instead go and see our uncle Geoffrey, who as it turns out had just fallen and dislocated his hip moments before we made our appearance and would love a hand getting up. When we are willing to go with the flow of things and trust our inner voice, we also get back onto the path of synchronicity where we know on a subtler level that what we are doing is just right.

If our ego mind still plays a large role in our creation, it will do all it can to try and halt our newfound ability by dismissing our inner voice as something irrational, crazy or just plain moronic. It will present us with what it thinks are hard-boiled facts to turn a blind eye to it and hurry us along our way. Tell it to chillax and take a moment to reconnect. If you have a habit of feeling confused and un-rooted in your Inner Self, invite mindfulness techniques into your life and count to 10 before insisting on making something happen in spite of all the arrows pointing towards a different direction.

It's also important to be aware of how much control we bestow on the people around us to call the shots in our life. Your own intuition can only be heard by you. Your mom, nana, best friend or sister cannot hear this voice, they can barely hear their own, so although they may have your best interest at heart, their own mind will try and project what they believe is right onto you— their fears will often get in the way of their better judgment. Resist the urge to follow someone else's direction. Although easier and seemingly less confusing, it will almost never lead you to where you need to be.

By honing our intuition and deepening our connection to our Inner Self, we open up a gateway of knowledge that is readily available to us at all times—we connect to the ever-present lifeline that assists us in taking spiritually-aligned decisions and make life that little bit easier. And with a little practice, there are a few things that you can do to get your connection with your heart back online.

Tip: If your link is a little rusty, it may be a good idea to fine-tune the strands so that an easier communication can flow openly and with less delay. During a meditation, try to ask a question to your heart. Sit with this question for a few moments and pay close attention to the medium your heart uses to communicate with you. This can vary from person to person. Do you see any colors pop up in the eye of your mind? Do you feel any pain/ twitch in your body? Can you hear any sounds? It may take a few practice sessions, but the more you try, the quicker you will be able to recognize its language.

The corner of Max: Max was getting good at listening to his gut feeling. He recognized the tell signs and its expression; although sometimes, even he got it mixed up with his own thought-process. Now too intuitive to dismiss such an internal communication flaw, he endeavored to find a pattern. As soon as his awareness shifted in its direction, he was able to catch how fear had been sneaking into the equation and see how it had favored the safety option in any decision making. His heart was often keen in jumping out into the unknown, but fear had unbeknownst to him still been strong. Luckily, as soon as he shined his LED flashlight in its eyes, fear cowardly ran under the carpet and out of the picture.

You already know. Listen to that knowing, it is there.

38

Integration: Blending spiritual nuts into the smoothie of your life

Truth is not something outside to be discovered, it is something inside to be realized.
~ Osho

Being spiritual in every aspect of life

Knowing a fundamental truth, versus actually integrating it as part of who we are, are two separate things. Many know the virtues on paper, but who is actually integrating these little seeds of knowledge into their daily lives? The mind can conceptually understand spiritual content, but it is your heart that will experientially integrate the wisdom into it. It's that integration that will bring the soul and the Self into the same box and force them to communicate and make a true difference to your life.

This applicability is best done by recognizing that spirituality is actually our entire life, to go down into the small stuff of our daily routines to understand that it is there that spirituality unfolds, not only when we feel good or are in the zone. Our lives are shaped continuously: when we stand in line at the supermarket and someone has just cut us; when we have just gotten fired and catch ourselves on the way to the bar; when we think no one is watching us go into a foul-mouthed rant. Every action, every thought contributes to who we are, always. You can't pause what you are creating, consciously or unconsciously, with awareness or without; the show will go on, so you might as well be fully in it.

As long as spirituality remains an intangible abstract notion, its integration will not be made possible; it will forever be something fluffy up there in the realm of philosophical chatter.

It is up to the individual to make the connection and embody it as part of who they are, thus allowing their true inner selves to mirror its pure essence.

Tip: Next time you read or hear something that resonates true to you, try to take the connection further by meditating over it. Can you begin to integrate that truth or notion and allow your Inner Self to feel it? When you hear someone say that "Love is all around you" and you find yourself nodding in agreement, can you connect to that part of you that knows how to actually experience that notion?

The corner of Max: Max had read nearly every holistic, self-development and esoteric book available on the market. He felt that he had acquired knowledge and spiritual wealth, although many of the topics were resonating truer on an intellectual level than from the context of his Inner Self. When super-aware Max made this observation, he set out to test every notion dear to his heart (such as forgiveness, honesty and authenticity) and integrate them with his being. This meant that he opened the door to situations and people that made these tests possible, from negative situations to challenging scenarios. Max knew when these moments arose, so next time a car drove into the back of his just as he was late for the theatre, he knew that the integration of patience was working through his system. Thank you, bad driver?

Every moment of your life counts in the grand scheme of your creation.

39

Rent-a-spiritual: The spiritual Ego

Enlightenment is ego's ultimate disappointment.
~ Chogyam Trungpa

How the Ego can manifest in spirituality

Nowadays many people brand themselves as 'spiritual' beings. The word gets tossed around a lot; though more often than not, its meaning becomes more on par to *supercalifragilisticexpialidocious* than anything half deep.

The rented-spiritualist likes to throw the occasional Om chant around, finish their e-mails with 'love and light' and their Facebook wall may be full of Osho quotes. Yet when it comes to their surroundings, they are more judgmental than your aunt Mildred. They often have a flair for courteously insulting you and are good at throwing you the 'I'm an old soul and you are not' card to make you feel like the loser who just walked in on an exclusive members' gathering. The spiritual ego makes them feel superior to their environment and you really have to pause and ask yourself why, instead of walking home with your bottom lip trembling.

Most people that fit this model are actually craving that famous self-love as much as anyone else—they have simply anchored themselves with yet another security blanket in the form of 'Spiritual' marketing; but that's all it is, another fear-based mechanism to be loved and respected from the outside.

The true legacy of a person lies in the way they make people feel in their presence. In the light there is no judgment or discrimination; there is no need to point out other people's weaknesses in order to make ourselves feel better, for we have already integrated the understanding that fundamentally we are all one.

Tip: If you meet feelings of superiority within your spiritual path, try to pause and ask yourself why this need is present. Does an external validation of your worth provide you with the reassurance that you seek?

The corner of Max: Every now and then, when Max would meet people who were still intent on living their lives with their fear goggles on, he would feel a subtle feeling of condescension creep up within him. At first it was almost untraceable; but as time went on, it became louder and more noticeable. He deduced that everyone did the same on some level, although in Max's heart, and now also mind, judging or categorizing others was not synonymous with love, and hence had no place in his being. From then on, every time he recognized that familiar feeling turning up, he would stop, observe it with scrutinizing eyes and thank it for being there, before releasing it altogether. It took some practice and a lot of dedication to finally ask himself why he would have the need to pass judgment on others in the first place. When he finally saw little Mr. Ego folded neatly in the corners of his mind, he noticed that it had its shoulders slightly raised, head cocked to one side as if to say: Come on, pal, what did you expect? Needless to say, little ego got grounded, with a strict round the clock curfew for weeks to come.

He who does not need external validations, is the most feared in the world.

40

Kindness is the new black

Be kind, for everyone you meet is fighting a hard battle.
~ Plato

The power of kindness on your spiritual journey

More and more people are becoming aware of their internal realities and how those are being mirrored with their external ones—from that unpleasant conversation with the barman to the unexpected promotion, every moment of your life is being pulled into your reality by you, good or bad, no one else is to blame. This alone is going to set off a mixture of mild anxiety and wondrous stupor as the underlying sense of duty and self-responsibility become one and the same.

Having this realization in itself is amazing, though many seem to forget how the quality of kindness fits into the equation. Knowing that we attract everything is not always easy to swallow, let alone trying to decipher the reason behind it. When Steve gets afflicted with a bad case of hemorrhoids, next time instead of answering with a stiff "well he attracted that onto himself", we should endeavor to bring compassion and kindness into the conversation. Being an interconnected species means that what is happening to your neighbor is affecting you, so their well-being is really yours; after all, that's what being empathetic really entails, to remember the You in others.

An act of kindness can not only uplift the other person, it can do wonders for you too. Kindness empowers, it takes you to places you could never reach in its absence, it allows you to see the light inside of yourself while spreading it further to all that you come into contact with like a magic blanket. Kindness is really the new cool. Forget about goody-two-shoes, I'm talking über hipster with the two dots above the U, the new fashion to be worn and adorned by every generation; and what's more, it's a trend that will never go out of style.

Kindness is a chameleon. It can take the shape of almost every action of your life, from the divine act of listening without the need to hear yourself fixing the other person's problem, to a random hug, a cup of tea or in the valor of asking a worn-out waitress how she feels when you can see she is teary-eyed. Kindness takes courage because reaching out of your comfort zone means uncertainty of what it can bring in return, so when you stop expecting something coming your way, anything else is just a bonus (that includes the old man telling you to mind your own business after you stopped his walking frame from rolling down the road—at the very least you can boast about having met Mr. Scrooge in the flesh).

Tip: How can you incorporate little acts of kindness in your everyday life?

The corner of Max: When Max looked at his own reflection on a Tuesday evening, he saw a changed man. There was little left of the impatient, greedy, unkind and self-obsessed man that had walked Earth a mere three years prior. Looking into his own eyes in the bathroom mirror, he saw a compassionate man that had awoken from a deep sleep. A man who no longer blamed the world for his own reality. A man who knew how to love and be loved, and who valued kindness as the new order of the day. When people would come to him for advice, he had the patience to be there for them and the kindness to listen. A round of applause to Max Hannigan, everyone.

When you put your fears, your prejudice and above all your ego aside, the act of listening becomes the highest form of a selfless act.

41

A new Speciation

Closing words

There is a new Earth in the making.

It's calling out right now to the brave, to the curious and to those who will no longer remain a slave.

It's adjuring her children to take their first steps towards a new dawn and disembark from the patriarchal ship of fear that for too long has kept them all in pernicious stasis. Part of a conscious speciation, these open-eyed individuals know that change is the new coin of the realm and they are not letting the consternation of uncertainty hold them back any longer.

They may be shunted out of the comfort of what once was, or ridiculed for embodying divergent ideas, but the calling towards their true potential is greater; it's innate and so clear because he who listens to his heart can hear the divine messages of all that is.

O-BOOKS

SPIRITUALITY

O is a symbol of the world, of oneness and unity; this eye represents knowledge and insight. We publish titles on general spirituality and living a spiritual life. We aim to inform and help you on your own journey in this life.

If you have enjoyed this book, why not tell other readers by posting a review on your preferred book site? Recent bestsellers from O-Books are:

Heart of Tantric Sex
Diana Richardson
Revealing Eastern secrets of deep love and intimacy to Western couples.
Paperback: 978-1-90381-637-0 ebook: 978-1-84694-637-0

Crystal Prescriptions
The A-Z guide to over 1,200 symptoms and their healing crystals
Judy Hall
The first in the popular series of six books, this handy little guide is packed as tight as a pill-bottle with crystal remedies for ailments.
Paperback: 978-1-90504-740-6 ebook: 978-1-84694-629-5

The 7 Myths about Love...Actually!
The journey from your HEAD to the HEART of your SOUL
Mike George
Smashes all the myths about LOVE.
Paperback: 978-1-84694-288-4 ebook: 978-1-84694-682-0

The Holy Spirit's Interpretation of the New Testament
A course in Understanding and Acceptance
Regina Dawn Akers
Following on from the strength of *A Course In Miracles*, NTI
teaches us how to experience the love and oneness of God.
Paperback: 978-1-84694-085-9 ebook: 978-1-78099-083-5

The Message of A Course In Miracles
A translation of the text in plain language
Elizabeth A. Cronkhite
A translation of *A Course in Miracles* into plain, everyday
language for anyone seeking inner peace. The companion
volume, *Practicing A Course In Miracles*, offers practical lessons
and mentoring.
Paperback: 978-1-84694-319-5 ebook: 978-1-84694-642-4

Thinker's Guide to God
Peter Vardy
An introduction to key issues in the philosophy of religion.
Paperback: 978-1-90381-622-6

Your Simple Path
Find happiness in every step
Ian Tucker
A guide to helping us reconnect with what is really important in
our lives.
Paperback: 978-1-78279-349-6 ebook: 978-1-78279-348-9

365 Days of Wisdom
Daily Messages To Inspire You Through The Year
Dadi Janki
Daily messages which cool the mind, warm the heart and guide
you along your journey.
Paperback: 978-1-84694-863-3 ebook: 978-1-84694-864-0

Body of Wisdom
Women's Spiritual Power and How it Serves
Hilary Hart
Bringing together the dreams and experiences of women across
the world with today's most visionary spiritual teachers.
Paperback: 978-1-78099-696-7 ebook: 978-1-78099-695-0

Practicing A Course In Miracles
A Translation of the Workbook in Plain Language and With
Mentoring Notes
Elizabeth A. Cronkhite
The practical second and third volumes of The Plain-Language
A Course In Miracles.
Paperback: 978-1-84694-403-1 ebook: 978-1-78099-072-9

Readers of ebooks can buy or view any of these bestsellers by
clicking on the live link in the title. Most titles are published
in paperback and as an ebook. Paperbacks are available in
traditional bookshops. Both print and ebook formats are
available online.
Find more titles and sign up to our readers' newsletter at
http://www.johnhuntpublishing.com/mind-body-spirit
Follow us on Facebook at https://www.facebook.com/OBooks/
and Twitter at https://twitter.com/obooks